50 WAYS TO

# SUCCEED
# MORE &
# SCREW
# UP
# LESS

Peter N. Fahrenkamp, MA

**A Journey to Self-Improvement,
Effective Communication, and Better
Relationships at Work and Home**

succeedmore@solutionbydesign.com
www.solutionbydesign.com/succeedmore

Printed and bound in the United States of America
ISBN: 979-8-218-53505-6

# Praise for *50 Ways to Succeed More & Screw Up Less*

"*Fifty Ways* is a masterpiece of original wisdom that is pithy, fun to read, and one profound insight after the other that will enhance your life."

—Warren Farrell, PhD,
Author of *The Boy Crisis* and *Role Mate to Soul Mate*

"Packed with uncommon wisdom, *50 Ways to Succeed More and Screw Up Less* is a practical field guide for well-being. Peter's insights provide a rare and fresh approach to handling life's challenges with grace and elegance. It's an uplifting read. If you've ever thought, 'There must be a better way,' this book is for you."

—Peter Meyers, CEO Stand & Deliver,
Author of *As We Speak*

"In this engaging and easily readable handbook, Peter Fahrenkamp shares insights on many of the most common issues faced by people all over the world on a daily basis. Using his unique style and wit, Peter speaks directly to the reader, providing actionable advice on a diverse range of topics, including communication styles, coping with difficult emotions, clarifying personal values, and more. Unlike many self-help books, this one is both a pleasure to read and bound to benefit the reader."

—Ryan Van Patten, PhD,
Assistant Professor, Brown University

"This little gem addresses so many dilemmas we all face, whether we're on our own or in a relationship. The concise and profound collection of insights offered by Peter will make you reflect and lead you to a better approach in your thinking as well as in your conversations with yourself and those you relate to. Nowhere else will you find a toolbox with so many great tools for all-around improvement. I have no doubt that your life will improve from these quick and lighthearted yet profound reads."

—Alan Ross, UC Berkeley Distinguished Teaching Fellow
Founder, Chris Kindness Award

# CALL TO ACTION

Can you think of other topics you wish
were included in this book?

Do you have unique observations and differing
experiences with certain topics?

Might you have any examples of how you positively
applied some of the book's content?

Let Peter know and he will respond.
succeedmore@solutionbydesign.com
www.solutionbydesign.com/succeedmore

# CONTENTS

## PART THREE: CONVERSATIONS WITH OTHERS

# FOREWORD

As a champion of positive human evolution individually and collectively, Peter shares his collection of *50 Ways to Succeed More and Screw Up Less* to improve ourselves, our communication, and our relationships both at home and at work. This book is designed to support us to evolve positively in the most important aspects of our lives. Sharing insights gained from his lifelong study of the human condition and from three decades of coaching people professionally, he shares his collected wisdom in a light, entertaining, yet profound fashion. His savvy perspectives and clear approaches guide us to be happier, more authentic, less judgmental, and more content with ourselves and those around us.

Each of the *50 Ways* is a brief and wise condensation of complex dynamics, and reading them will simply and effectively empower us and our relationships. When one person evolves, we all benefit, and when one relationship improves, we all benefit. While addressing deep topics in a concise fashion, these *50 Ways* point us in incredibly helpful and upbeat directions. Peter's *50 Ways* to improve ourselves, our communication, and our relationships are offered in *four* important areas of our lives.

Part One is about the conversations we have with the person we spend the most time with—ourselves! Our many *conversations with ourselves* set the fundamental tone of our life. While most of us feel that this tone is not ours to manage, the reality is that it is *all* ours to manage. Learning how to separate and manage our own thoughts and emotions opens doorways to more internal choice and fosters our emotional and mental equilibrium. Regardless of what our circumstances may be, this section offers deep insights and simple ways in which we can recognize and exercise more choice to powerfully set the tone of our own mind, our own emotions, and our life.

Part Two of the book deals with how we handle *our own challenging emotions*. Face it, life triggers us often, and the more observant we become both of ourselves and of others, the more options we have, and the more proactive and constructive we can be in any situation. Discovering healthy ways to handle challenging emotions will result in becoming less reactive, less dramatic, and calmer. Identifying and separating our responsibilities from those of others allows our internal life to become easier to manage. In doing so, relationships become healthier and life becomes less of an emotional roller coaster and more of a peaceful journey.

Part Three addresses our *conversations with others*. As we all know, relationships can be a challenge, but they can also be a great source of happiness when we are in quality, enjoyable, and solid relationships with our closest people both at home and at work. With the perspectives offered in this area, we will know how to communicate more effectively, listen better, and give feedback in a way that is both easier to deliver *and* easier to hear. When we have more effective conversations with others, we become better parents, colleagues, partners, leaders, neighbors, friends, children, and siblings. And when we are able to have challenging conversations in kind, clear, and elegant ways, relationships can become easier.

Part Four of the book looks at our *challenging relational emotions,* including challenging topics such as boundaries, love, power struggles, bullying, and being a victim. It is often our closest relationships both at home and at work that cause the toughest challenges. Becoming a wiser and better version of ourselves, we will also become easier for others to relate to. Peter's guidance in this section clears up the confusion we often face when our relational emotions are running high and offers positive direction that creates clarity and a more grounded way of handling the tough interpersonal times in our closest relationships.

Peter's *50 Ways to Succeed More and Screw Up Less* allow us to bypass our ego-based way of living and instead enable us, one step at a time, to be able to think, feel, speak, and behave in clearer and more effective ways. Functioning with less ego will help us have more choice in all aspects of our life and we can become more joy-filled. Although it would be easy to consume the *50 Ways* in one sitting, it's best for us to take the time to read <u>one topic at a time</u>. Read one and ponder it. When we put the various insights and learnings into action in our world, notice how it impacts us, our life, and the lives of those around us.

"*Do the best you can until you know better. Then when you know better, do better,*" the American memoirist, poet, and civil rights activist Maya Angelou once said. So as we do better by implementing what we glean from these *50 Ways to Succeed More and Screw Up Less,* pass this little yet powerful book on to others. Imagine what the world would be like if we share these *50 Ways* with our partner, our friends, family, and work colleagues; we'll make our world better and the world of those around us better too.

**Lorin Beller**

*Author, professional coach, inspirer for the human spirit to continue to evolve, and champion of Peter's work.*

# INTRODUCTION

When my friend Anne-Louise and I caught up over lunch, she shared her frustration about some of her friends having just given her a bunch of (unsolicited) advice about how to manage her finances. My response was "Oh, they didn't get the memo!?" "No, they didn't get the memo," my friend said. Lamenting the prevalence of unsolicited advice in life, we had a wistful conversation about there not being a handbook, a collection of helpful memos, a compilation of fundamentally important insights which one could just read or give to others as a present. "Why don't you and I write that book together!?" I exclaimed. "*You* write it," Anne-Louise said—and so I did. This is that book.

*50 Ways to Succeed More and Screw Up Less* is written for ultraconservatives and raging left-wingers, for millennials and boomers, for swingers and priests, for janitors and CEOs, for narcissists and victims, for millionaires and paupers—in other words, it's written for you and me. How you identify in life doesn't matter here, because the thinking presented in this book doesn't concern itself with adherence to dominant societal beliefs, established morals or values, cultural movements, or political correctness. While it doesn't dismiss any of those, it doesn't blindly endorse them either.

We all have two kinds of relationships—those with ourselves and those with others. Generally, we focus almost exclusively on the relationships we have with others. However, long before and long after we talk to others, we talk to ourselves—and we do that *a lot*. In fact, we have hundreds of mostly silent conversations with ourselves every day, regardless of how much we engage with others. It's easy to overlook or underestimate these internal conversations, but they are the very foundation from which we engage with the world around us. These conversations with ourselves mostly happen unconsciously, and it is equally unconsciously that they inform our thinking and especially our beliefs. Thus these 50 topics focus on two kinds of conversations—those we have with ourselves and those we have with others.

After you've been through a tough situation yourself and you've gotten clarity in hindsight, have you ever thought, "I wish I had understood this earlier"? Or have you ever gone through a challenging encounter with someone else and thought to yourself, "I wish they'd get it"? Or have you found yourself saying to yourself, "I wish I knew how to not sabotage myself and my relationships." If so, this book is for you. It's about the insights and understandings we wish we would have gotten earlier, or that others would have gotten before they put us through whatever arduous process we had to endure with them. And you might know someone who's dealing with certain topics addressed in this book, and you might do them a favor by sharing one or the other topic with them. Friends helping friends is great.

We all want to behave like good people, do the right thing, and get along, and most of us want to believe that we're pretty evolved. Yet, sometimes we just have a hard time with ourselves, we don't get along, we don't do the right thing, we don't behave like good people, and we sure don't act particularly enlightened. Life can present us with many unforeseen twists and turns and we often feel unprepared, don't know what to do, or are plain lost. Issues that present themselves in our relationships—with ourselves or with others—can often feel unclear, frustrating, or just too damn complicated. Sometimes when things go sideways we don't know how we got there, and we don't know how to make any sense of what's happening—especially when what's happening has repeated itself over and over. While we don't want to, we often fail ourselves and each other—we screw up in little and in big ways. And we all know that during times of unawareness or stress, we *don't* show up as our best selves.

Life is complex, we are complex, and often it is too hard or takes too long to understand complex topics. We don't have the time, the interest, the attention span, or the discipline to dive deep. These *50 Ways* address seemingly complex topics with concision, brevity, and clarity while offering understanding, helpful insights, and the kind of practical pointers we'd love to have when it counts. None of us *want* to screw up our lives or our relationships, yet we often do. Most of us want to be successful, but we don't always succeed. And sometimes succeeding may just mean screwing up a little less. Wouldn't it be great if in times of confusion, conflict, or when we're up a certain creek with no paddle, there was a compilation of fundamentally important topics we could consult that would allow us to act just a little more sane or evolved?

If you're anything like me, then you've screwed things up at times without knowing why, or just didn't know how to succeed more—both within yourself and within your relationships. Studying the human condition for my entire adult life, and having professionally coached many people in business and personal matters, I've come across certain fundamental topics time and again. Each time I've gained a bit more awareness, a bit more clarity, and have done a bit more research. Each time I understood *more*, created a little more peace within myself, communicated a bit more effectively, and had a little more success at relationships both at work and at home. So often when I've finally understood something I've thought to myself, "If I had only known this earlier, I would have screwed up less and been more successful." I am offering this collection of *50 Ways to Succeed More and Screw Up Less* so that you may save some time, all the while developing a better understanding of the world inside you, a better understanding of how to communicate more effectively, and a better understanding of how to be more successful in relationships both at work and at home.

Enjoy quick, independent reads of a few minutes each that may help you gain more insight into yourself and your relationships. These *50 Ways* may help you become more aware and conscious, communicate more effectively, and manage to have healthier and more successful relationships. Each topic stands on its own; i.e., no topic is needed to read and understand any other topic, although some later topics may reference notions which are addressed in earlier topics. If some topics or perspectives seem controversial, check in with your own true experiences and observations before you dismiss them. Check out which topics speak to you and take a few minutes to take the thinking presented for a spin. Have a look at where it might apply in your life or in the lives of those you care about. Each topic will take about as long to read as it took to read this introduction. Have fun with it. Try having a new and maybe more successful conversation with yourself or with those around you!

## CONVERSATIONS
## WITH OURSELVES

We have hundreds, if not thousands, of conversations with ourselves every day. Nobody else hears them, and most of them even we are not conscious of. Yet none of us were ever taught how to have these conversations in helpful ways—how to keep our minds and hearts operating smoothly, with clarity, simplicity, effectiveness, and elegance. And society's influence doesn't help us very much with the health of our internal conversations. Here are some key insights that might come in handy toward improving the conversations we have with ourselves, and toward running a well-honed mental and emotional system.

# HAPPINESS VS. CONTENTMENT

The former American Justice Potter Stewart once said, "I may not be able to define pornography, but I know it when I see it." This holds true for happiness—it's hard to define, but we know it when we feel it. And we all seek it and pursue it. Happiness may be easily confused with states of joy or euphoria. So just what is happiness, and how well do we all do in pursuing and attaining it? And what about contentment? Is that boring? Let's look at what happiness is first.

Happiness could be described as a momentary emotion of unconflicted joy when one feels, in the moment, that one's life is heading toward its desired course. It's a place, a moment, when all one's values are in harmony with one's experience. It's a state without suspicion or resentment toward others, and without living in the past or in the future. It's the state when one's mental, physical, and emotional capacities are effective and fully engaged in the realization of one's life.

It's interesting that one cannot aim directly for happiness, as it is an *effect*—a reaction to some particular thing or event or chain of events. One could say that happiness is a positive and joyful feeling *this* side of euphoria. A state without conflicting thoughts or conflicting values, when absolutely nothing is lacking in terms of needs or desires. When things are 100% *enough*, when we feel fully alive with nothing amiss, and nothing missing.

This of course is a tall order, and few of us often feel that nothing is lacking, that there's no conflict, and especially no contradiction in thoughts and feelings. It's rare, and for some of us, it's entirely elusive. Yet, we so easily ask one another, "Are you happy?" Why such a tall order of a question? And don't we feel a tiny bit of pressure to say yes? Because if we say no—then what? Happiness seems wonderful to pursue, to have as a guiding star, but how attainable and especially *sustainable* is it for most of us?

*The pursuit of happiness can be like a craving for joy. Cravings and their satiation, however, are short-lived.*

Let's look at contentment and how it compares to happiness. Contentment means you have a fairly constant and continuous experience of life, one without radical highs, but also without radical lows. While there may well be spikes of happiness, the majority of one's experience may be *a consistent wave of contentment.* You plan some, but you remain spontaneous and flexible. When you encounter setbacks, you don't immediately forget all the things that *are* working for you. You appreciate where you've come from and how far you've gotten in life.

The basics in your life—such as food, shelter, work, and relationships—are covered in an acceptable fashion. You have things that you look forward to and you have things you like to remember. You can appreciate the big things and the little things in your life. When matters aren't going your way, you aren't completely thrown off course. You consider things thoughtfully and keep reactivity to a minimum. Your very low level of anxiety keeps you from making rash decisions. There are great times and less great times. You could have more money, but you could also have less. You don't ride high and fall low—you're pretty constant.

> A sense of contentment is a solid foundation for moments of happiness.

This may sound boring when compared to happiness, and many of us wouldn't want to "settle" for "just" being content. Most of us have gotten used to a mentality that always wants more—more freedom, more money, more this and more that. But what is enough? When is it enough? Most of us don't have great answers to those questions.

Someone once said, "The meaning of money is that I don't have enough of it." Could the desire for and the expectation of happiness be *too much*, maybe even a trap that's always on the horizon but never quite arrives?

It's quite possible that as we pursue the elusive state of happiness, we overlook the possibility of steady and more attainable contentment. Most of us race forward, ahead, into the future, eyes on the prize, wanting bigger, better, and more. We forget that highs *require* lows in order to qualify for highs. Most of us want less drama in our life, less ups followed by downs, less elation followed by despair. Couldn't that sound pretty good—a state of humming along steadily through life, realizing it's not all good and not all bad, not all highs and not all lows?

What about life with less regrets, less reactivity, more acceptance, and a profound realization that things are pretty good and that they surely could be a hell of a lot worse? Would you forgo occasional or rare moments of true happiness for many moments of contentment? Would you spend $500 a year on lottery tickets in hopes you might win big? Or would you spend that $500 on something that will support your life, or even spend it on someone else? Isn't it great to have choices in how we handle the many twists and turns in life? Some of us will pursue happiness, others will pursue contentment. It takes all kinds.

Happiness is fleeting. Contentment is stable.

For most of us, happiness is dependent on things going well. Happiness vanishes when times get tough. Happiness is an emotional reaction to external events or some sort of stimulation. Contentment, on the other hand, is fairly independent of how things are going. The experience can stay even when the going gets tough, because contentment is not dependent on external events or stimulation. It's safer, more attainable, more solid, more sustainable, and it stays with us even when the outside world doesn't collaborate with our expectations and desires. Give it a think.

# YOUR THOUGHTS ARE
# NOT YOUR FEELINGS

n practice, we blend thoughts and feelings to such a degree that we often can't tell the difference. When asked what we feel, we often answer with what we think, and when asked what we think, we often answer with what we feel. There's lots of confusion about thoughts and feelings.

It's hard to separate thoughts and feelings.
But it's well worth it.

Our thinking can be off or distorted, yet our feelings can feel so damn true. When we mix distorted and automatic thinking with feelings, we have a mess. And because we often have strong feelings about our thoughts, they often *feel* real, which adds to the confusion. As it turns out, *feelings make thoughts seem real.* But this is an illusion: thoughts are *not* real! They only *feel* real. If you recognize that your thoughts are not real, you will be able to dismiss distorted, unhelpful thoughts—and may opt to *feel* better.

> Your thoughts are not your feelings.
> Feelings make them seem real.

This is tricky, yet it's possible. Identify your distorted thinking—here are some examples. Do you see things in black and white, all-or-nothing categories? Do you jump to conclusions without having hard facts? Do you magnify or minimize the importance of things? Do you focus on single negative details and dwell on them? Do you disqualify positive experiences in order to maintain a negative outlook?

Do you motivate yourself with *should* statements? Do you assign motive to others without having sure knowledge? Do you argue emotionally (it feels true, therefore it must be true)?

---

Ask yourself:

What are my thoughts about these feelings?

---

We all suffer from some degree of distorted thinking. Identifying our default distortions can be extremely helpful so that we can catch ourselves when we make the critical error of *mistaking* our thoughts for our feelings. *Separating thoughts from feelings* solves a lot of seemingly real problems and can keep us from spiraling downward and entering a vicious cycle.

Thoughts are not real. You can dismiss
distorted thoughts and opt to feel better.

Once you have identified distorted thoughts, you can counter them with more reasoned, sober, and balanced counterarguments. It's critical that you don't do that in your mind (remember, it's your mind that tricked you into a downward spiral in the first place!); instead, it's *necessary* that you do this *in writing*. Writing things out is the first step toward liberating us from the cyclical thought patterns of our mind, and helps us to *see with sobriety* when our thinking is distorted. Treat your thoughts as if they are outside yourself—observe them, write them down, and see how helpful or true they are. Often, you will find that they are neither.

> If you feel anxious, that doesn't mean that *you are* anxious. It means you are experiencing the symptoms of anxiety, not that you *are* anxiety.

This counterbalancing of automatic thoughts reduces our anxiety almost immediately. Try it out. Over time, as we practice this internal re-education, we can respond to unsettling events in more and more balanced and reasonable ways. And once we identify certain ways of thinking as not real, we can then *choose* to feel better about things.

# BEING RIGHT IS A LONELY PLACE

ost of us enjoy being right; however, being *right* usually entails someone else being *wrong*. Being right or wrong even in the conversations we have with ourselves is like saying that there's only one true color, and that it's either red or green. We know better than that, but are often seduced into wanting to be right so that our worth, our value, and our identity get bolstered a bit. We want to save face and we don't want to appear stupid, clueless, or uneducated.

We don't enjoy *being wrong*. Most of us already feel like there's something fundamentally wrong with us, and that belief can nudge us even further toward avoiding being wrong. We want to be "right" in some fashion, about some things, some of the time, and while that is understandable, does it really help our self-worth and our relationships?

We may not be conscious of it, but when we talk about being right and being wrong, we are coming from an emotional place—a place where judgments and opinions are at home. And everybody comes to the table with their own judgments and opinions, which means that as long as we stay with our emotions about what we believe is right and wrong, we're gearing up for a subtle—or not so subtle—fight about who's right and who's wrong.

This always includes someone losing, and since we hate to lose, we may at times insist on being right even beyond what we're sure of. We may even put forth "facts" we're quickly dreaming up in the moment, in order to not have to admit that we're wrong. Even if being right pumps us up momentarily and gives us the illusion of value and worth, deep down we know that it leaves us alone, that it disconnects us rather than connects us, that it doesn't nourish but instead diminishes our relationships and our sense of belonging.

Being right always means someone is feeling wrong.
Being accurate can leave everybody feeling right.

Luckily, there's another option to being right and to avoiding being wrong. We can be *accurate*. Being accurate is a matter of being factual, and being factual is not an emotional process. As such, being accurate—or inaccurate—is not a matter of judgment or opinion, which can liberate us from the unhelpful "one true color" perspective that being right inevitably presents us with. We all make errors, all of our memories are flawed, and all of our perceptions are just that—perceptions— so it's entirely normal and acceptable to at times be accurate and at other times be inaccurate. Being accurate or inaccurate is much healthier nourishment for our minds and hearts, and the minds and hearts of others, than being right or wrong is.

Bringing facts to conversations is significantly more helpful than bringing our emotions to them—even to the conversations we have with ourselves, in our minds. Emotions fluctuate, facts don't. How we feel often needs to be controlled, while facts don't require any maintenance at all—they just *are*. Being factual is helpful for our own sanity long before we bring issues to conversations with others. Looking at facts, and facts only, keeps us from taking involuntary emotional hikes that set us up for either losing or winning. Relationships are not about winning or losing; they are about nourishment, about connection, about safety, and about belonging.

If you want to be alone, be right.
If you want to be in relationship, be accurate.

Being right and being wrong are almost built into the very fabric of the way we are and the way we speak—and yet, they polarize us. To make matters worse, we tend to say "you're wrong" rather than "what you said is wrong"—thus paving the way for the listener to take the unhelpful shortcut toward there being something wrong with *them*. Being right and wrong are high stakes and they plug into our fickle emotions in unnecessary ways. Talking about what's accurate or inaccurate, however, can decrease the stakes and help make a conversation more calm and level-headed. If being right and being wrong are heavy like hammers, then being accurate and being inaccurate are light like nails. Nobody gets accused of "being wrong" when one person voices what they believe to be accurate.

Give it a try in the conversations you have in your mind first, then give it a try in conversations with others. See if you can wean yourself from the entrenched notions of *being right* and *being wrong*. See if you can put those old ideas to sleep while you wake up new ideas around being *factual, accurate*, and maybe even *correct*. Try introducing accuracy and inaccuracy into your conversations. See how it allows you to stay calm emotionally and have a clearer mind. Emotional and mental equilibrium is a fantastic experience. And those around you will be grateful to you for not making them feel that they are wrong!

# STOP TRYING TO MEDITATE!

Meditating is known to have great value and many benefits, but for many, learning how to meditate is daunting and hard, and success can be hard to measure or attain. There appears to be a popular belief that meditating entails *sitting still*, *not thinking*, and *quieting one's mind*. And while it *sounds* relatively easy to just sit, *quiet the mind*, *not think*, and *do nothing*, it proves to be quite hard for almost all of us. This popular and unquestioned belief is so commonplace that most of us never question if we're going about this in a helpful manner. Shouldn't it at least give us pause for thought that it's *so damn hard* to not think—to quiet the chatter in our mind?

Those who are "successful" at meditation report many great by-products, such as feeling centered, calm, present, attentive, grounded, and achieving a sense of serenity. As it turns out, the biggest issue with learning how to meditate is that we're *trying*—trying what appears to be so hard to do. This *trying* gets exacerbated by believing that we need all sorts of accoutrements in order to "do it right." We get all tangled up in believing that we need silence, the right background music, the right teacher, or the right time, location, or even sitting position. It's a lot—and we're still *trying*. Most of us find it hard, and many of us feel that we just can't do it—we "fail." Actually, the door to meditation can open quite easily when we cease to *try*.

> Trying is an activity. See what happens when you simply stop trying.

When you're *trying* to be centered, you're not centered. When you're *trying* to stop your restless mind, your mind is not quiet. When you're *trying* to focus on your breathing, you're not just breathing. When you're *trying* to tune out the background noise, you're hearing the background noise. However, when you're *not trying*, when you're just *noticing* and *observing* what's going on, *then* it turns out *you're centered*. When you're watching your restless mind, witnessing what it's doing, *then* your mind will quiet down. When you're *observing* your breathing, regardless of how even or stifled or shallow or deep it may be—*then* you're allowing yourself to *just* breathe. You are, in essence, just *acknowledging what is*.

The magic to meditation is to remove the *trying* and the *incessant judging*—most likely the judging of doing something *wrong*. The only "wrong" thing about meditation is the trying. There's always plenty to notice when you're meditating without *trying* anything—there are thoughts, sounds, smells, bodily sensations, and *more* thoughts. And all there is to *do* is to *observe* everything that's going on. There is nothing else to *do*. Try it—you might find that your awareness can witness, observe, or notice layers upon layers of sensations, thoughts, thoughts about sensations, sensations about thoughts, thoughts about thoughts, and so on. There's an almost never-ending number of things to notice or observe, and *noticing* or *observing* is all there is to do.

"No deed there is, no doer thereof."

There's a multiverse inside all of us waiting to be explored, to be noticed, to be observed. The key to meditation is to *avoid nothing*—only notice, observe, witness—and with a little practice, what you experience will amount to a serene observed experience of your inner reality. Even if that inner reality is chaotic or overwhelming, even if you have incessant inner dialogue or lots of negative thoughts—the part of you that *watches* it all is a steady, serene part of your Self. Regardless of what transpires, *that* part of yourself just *is,* without needing to *do* anything. You don't even have to find that part of your Self—it will find you the moment you stop *trying,* the moment you simply notice, observe, and witness all that's going on inside you. And this somewhat detached or dispassionate "activity" can be a very peaceful experience.

> The trick is to watch and observe your thoughts—rather than *follow* them.

When you watch your thoughts, feelings, or sensations, the big seduction is to *follow* those thoughts, feelings, or sensations—and next thing you know, you are only *thinking.* *This* is the major challenge—to return to just *observing* your thoughts rather than getting swept up by them. This takes practice! See if you can spend a few seconds, then a few minutes, just observing your thoughts, your feelings, your sensations. See if you can *find* the moment, the "place" where you get swept up in your thoughts or feelings. The moment when you *notice* that you've been taken hostage by your thoughts or feelings, witness yourself noticing this, and then continue to just *notice* and *witness* all that is going on in your mind, your heart, your soul, your body—in *you*. It won't take long before you'll be able to identify and get to know *that* place from which you can just *observe*. It is a big goal already to practice this *unattached* or *dispassionate* experiencing of your own thoughts and feelings.

Specifically, if you find that criticism and judgment take over, notice the criticism and the judgment. It's key to *not try* to stop it—just observe it arise and then observe it go its way. Then other thoughts will present themselves, or your "observing" will generate some of its own. There's no need to stop or try anything—just keep watching and observing—that's *all* there is to do. When you watch your thoughts, you *are* no longer your thoughts. When you watch your feelings, you are no longer your feelings. Watching them changes the power equation between *you* and your thoughts or feelings—they won't control you any longer. It can almost be *fun* to watch what your mind will cook up and present you with. Amazingly, watching or observing *in itself* can be a calming behavior.

When you watch your thoughts,
you are no longer your thoughts.

Maybe the simplest way to paraphrase meditating would be to call it *the activity of being present*—paying attention to what's going on in each moment. Forget about needing a quiet place, the "right" sitting position, or any environmental constraints. Close your eyes for a few seconds or minutes—on the bus, in the shower, in bed—and discover hitherto unknown parts of your own inner self. Just notice, watch, and observe. The attention you devote to meditation could change your life.

# INTERNAL VS. EXTERNAL AUTHORITY

There are two kinds of authority we're motivated by—*internal* and *external* authority. Basically, being motivated by internal authority means we trust our own senses (information from the inside), and being motivated by external authority means we trust other people's senses (outside information). As children, we're dependent on parents and others for "informed" authority on life because we haven't experienced enough life yet on our own. As we mature, we develop that inner sense, an inner resource, which becomes *internal authority*. This means developing and trusting our senses, our intuition, our hunches, our gut reaction, our own belief systems, principles, worldviews, and our convictions.

As adults, there are lots of institutions that are essentially *external authority* that we are reasonably expected to follow and obey, such as laws, law enforcement, and the general rules governing life in groups and in society. At the same time, it is our inner compass that guides us through *our life as humans*—it's our individual and internal source for decision-making, judgment calls, and for handling such basic feelings as trust, fear, curiosity, and interests.

It's a delicate process to develop our inner sense of such important decisions as what's good, what's right, what's dangerous, what's true, and what's trustworthy. It takes a lot of awareness of those in more responsible positions—external authorities—to balance what's truly needed in terms of guidance from the outside while allowing those still developing access to their own senses to do so, trusting that they will develop okay without unnecessary influence from the outside.

Being motivated from the inside, from *internal authority*, always competes with the motivations, rewards, recognitions, and feedback *external authorities* provide us with. Early on in education, children learn that there are right and wrong answers and behaviors—regardless of their own experience. Often, children learn to please adults in order to receive validation, and at times, even love. If this happens consistently, they begin to look outside themselves for love and approval. For instance, if adults praise young girls for the cute outfit they're wearing, how beautiful they are, or comment on their figure, girls learn that people give them love and approval based on their appearance and that certain looks or body types are more valued than others.

When this sort of conditioning by external authorities happens *at the expense* of acknowledging and validating the child's internal experiences, it can set us on a lifelong trajectory to basically forget or override our internal experiences altogether. In such cases, we may increasingly rely on external sources for our sense of identity and self-worth. We may rely on others for even basic experiences such as *how we feel*.

Many of our established institutions facilitate such reliance on external sources of authority. Organized religion, the news, entertainment and advertising industries, all present themselves to us as external authorities who *purport to know better* than we do—know better what to believe, what to idealize, whose information to trust, what products to buy, and who to get ahead of in order to be successful. Add social media and we're also being told by others—usually people *we don't know*—how to look, what to wear, what to say, what to read, where to go on vacation; in short—how to *be.* The majority of those sources of *external authority* are pervasive in most of our lives.

---

*External authority* also means you don't have to take responsibility and are not accountable.

---

As a modern adult, it can be very hard to differentiate between messages that come from outside and messages that come from inside. It can result in struggling to identify and meet our own needs, self-validating our experiences, and can exacerbate our reactivity to external disapproval of us or of our decisions. It can become very easy to lose our sense of balance, basic okay-ness, and self-worth. Worse, it can lead to disorders, anxiety, or depression.

Modern life has the notion of *conditional approval* basically built-in. Most of us never even question such commonly held beliefs as *believing that we are only worthy if we are productive*. Or *believing* that we need people to like us in order to be a good person. Or *believing* that we are valued more when we do well in school or at work. Not that many things in modern Western society foster the development of *internal authority*. To be clear, cultivating trust in an internal authority doesn't automatically mean denying external authorities, or that we suddenly give ourselves over to every sensation and itch we feel.

There's tremendous value in being able to *identify what we're feeling*, learn to trust our body's sensations, learn to trust our minds, and not *mindlessly* going along with what peers, the media—other people in general—are suggesting, saying, or at times, even asking for or demanding. There's nothing lost when we learn to listen to ourselves and run the ideas of external authorities by our own internal authority. There's a lot gained from becoming less susceptible to what others think, say, suggest, or demand. The development of internal authority is one of the most critically important human features so many of us have lost. Find yours. It has almost all the answers.

Growing up also means
trusting your own judgment.

# THE POWER OF ANY TIME BUT NOW

Much has been written about the power of being present, the power of being here and now, about how the present is actually the only time we have—that the past is gone and the future isn't here yet. Still, most of us spend an inordinate amount of time remembering or lamenting yesterday, and hoping for or worrying about tomorrow. It seems built into us to forget all about the here and now and live our lives suspended between what is behind us and what is in front of us.

It is true that if we let go of preoccupying ourselves with yesterday and tomorrow, and if we focus only on *right now*, most of our worries won't have a leg to stand on. From misery over depression to anxiety, most negative emotional states *rely* on us spending our present time either in the past or in the future—or in both. Yesterday and tomorrow are huge distractions from being alive and present in the only moment we truly have, this one now. It raises the question of why yesterday and tomorrow are apparently more interesting to us than the present.

Many of us feel blue at times and get nervous at times. In other words, many of us suffer from occasional or frequent mild depressive states, and many of us suffer from occasional or frequent anxious states. Usually, depression and anxiety are not linked, as both manifest so differently. Anxiety appears as high-strung nerves and instability. Depression appears as low-strung nerves and stability, albeit unhappy stability. Interestingly, depression and anxiety are *two faces of the same coin*: anxiety concerns itself with perceived loss in the future, while depression concerns itself with perceived loss in the past.

Anxiety concerns itself with perceived loss in the future, while depression concerns itself with perceived loss in the past.

In addition to remembering great times gone by, we do spend a lot of our (present) time lamenting what happened in the past. And in addition to looking forward to tomorrow, we also spend a lot of our (present) time fretting about what's ahead. If one were able to remove the preoccupation with what *wasn't* in the past and with what *might not be* in the future, a lot of space and room would open up to us. That space and room would then be available to us *here, now, today,* for *this* moment. Being present would be so much easier were we not so prone to lament the past and fret about the future.

What often draws us away from the here and now is some level of fear—fear of having lost out in the past or fear of losing out in the future. The power of any time but now is a great power—it pulls us backward and forward at the same time. This somewhat irresistible power makes it hard for us to *stay* in the here, *stay* in the now, stay present. If—and that's a big if—we're able, just for a moment, to forget about what could have been and forget about what might be, then we can have an absolutely amazing experience of being present, here, now, in this moment. In those rare moments, almost nothing is missing, and unless we're in actual physical pain *right now*, any pain coming from a perceived past or future loss would have no leg to stand on.

---

Nothing beats being here and now
and nowhere else, even for a few seconds.

---

This is not easy to achieve, as evidenced by how much literature exists about how to be present and about the power of being here, now. Yet, it *is* possible to achieve such momentary states. The wonderful thing is that it doesn't take hundreds of those momentary experiences in order for us to *get it*—to get what it takes to *not* be suspended between yesterday and tomorrow, but instead to be *present*, to be *here*, and to do so *now*. Even if we only have this experience once or twice, it is an incredibly powerful experience, one well worth contemplating and experimenting with.

# GOOD INTENTIONS PAVE BAD ROADS

Oh, how we love good intentions. How often have we heard things like "But he meant well" or "She had nothing but good intentions"? When explaining or defending something that went sideways, we invoke *good intentions* so often that it would suggest that *bad intentions* are a realistic option. But how many people do you associate with who you know have *bad intentions*? Good intentions are pretty much a given among most of us.

Think about it. When things go sideways, we use the *good intentions* argument to justify a lot. As if the goodness of the intentions somehow mitigates the poorness of the actions. It's like a band-aid that makes us temporarily not see the wound; it's an excuse so that we don't have to have unpleasant confrontations.

> The sobering secret about *good intentions* is that they often cover up poor or lacking actions.

Of course we all want to mean well, and most of us do almost all the time. So, if you take intentions out of the equation, you're left with *actions*. And aren't those the things—the things that actually *happen*—that count at the end of the day? Wouldn't a focus on actions be more helpful than a focus on intentions? The old adage "Talk is cheap, actions are priceless" has a lot to offer.

> The road to *hell* is paved with good intentions.

Why do we, as people, so readily and often forget that terrible things are often committed with good intentions? Good intentions, when acted upon, can often have unintended negative consequences. And remember that having the intention to do good things—yet failing to take action due to procrastination or laziness—yields pretty much … nothing. Good *intentions* solve almost nothing. Good *actions,* however, can solve a lot of things. Forget your intentions. Focus on your actions.

The road to *heaven* is paved with good actions.

The next time you hear yourself or someone else saying "but they meant well" or "I know you had good intentions," take a moment to reflect on just why we apparently *have to* invoke good intentions. How is the situation or how are we served by painting over a lamentable situation with the brush of good intentions? How would we feel if we could not help ourselves to the good intentions brush? This is not an easy consideration, but it is a worthwhile one. We'd all benefit from focusing on actions over intent. And it's not impolite to call a spade a spade.

# ASSIGNING MOTIVE TO OTHERS

" I know exactly why she did it!" "It's totally clear what he wanted to accomplish!" We all know such statements. So often, *we know* what others meant or intended. We're sure of it. We don't even need to ask. We can just tell. And it relieves internal pressure to assign motive. We might feel righteous and we might even feel indignant! It surely takes us off the hook from having to ask and find out. But how did we become such great mind readers and fortune-tellers? How are we so sure of others' motives?

Once we clearly think and talk about it, it becomes self-evident that assigning meaning or motive to the actions of others is not helpful. It's not helpful because not only might we be wrong, but we then don't give others their chance to share where they're coming from. And we usually leave various possibilities unexamined and draw massive conclusions (usually negative ones) from the motives we have just assigned to others. We interpret wildly, we use singular lenses, and we disempower others. And we keep the focus *off* ourselves, as it's so much easier to talk about someone else negatively than about our own—likely anxious—evoked experience. Almost nothing about this is helpful at all.

Assigning motive doesn't reduce one's anxiety.

Let's take calling someone "manipulative." This is a negative label, not a compliment; it's neither neutral nor objective language. It's interpretive, subjective, and it overlooks perspectives that might be possible without this label. *It is a disempowering statement to the person who makes it as it implies or creates victimhood.* It leads one to interpret future behavior negatively. Ultimately, it's often not much more than a negative projection that *appears* to be self-serving; however, in reality it is actually self-sabotaging.

So little is good about assigning motive that it becomes a tremendously valuable exercise to see if one can do it *less*. The next time someone complains to you about what someone *else* apparently did, and especially *why* they did it, see if you can *avoid* taking sides. See if you can instead find out how the person doing the projection *feels*. It is so much more relevant and fruitful to talk about the feelings of someone who's right in front of you than to talk about people who aren't present. See if you can avoid getting roped into the triangle whose subtext reads, "If I tell you how ill-intentioned someone else is, then you'll side with me."

Assigning motive isn't much more
than a negative projection.

Do yourself and the person in front of you a favor by remaining impartial. See if you can avoid colluding with the "victim of the moment." Keep the focus on the person with the strong emotional experience; *be there for them* and what is going on for them. Chances are, it's possibly quite unrelated to the intent or motive of whoever is not present in your conversation. Look and see what is in front of you—likely a momentarily suffering person who has confused *experiencing* with *projecting*.

The ability to look and see clearly does *not* entail assigning motive. Try to avoid the pull of negative past experiences and negative future projections—yours or those of others. Look and see how to enhance your ability to notice, to perceive, and to be present. Ask questions when you're not clear. See if you can help separate fact from fiction and fact from feelings. Your friends will thank you for it, as we all would like our friends to stay present with us with as little judgment as possible.

# JUDGING (YOUR) PAST BY TODAY'S STANDARDS

We all do it: we judge historical events—whether from yesterday or fifty years ago—with today's standards, ethics, morals, and worldviews. We can't judge the future, and even the present can only be judged once the moment has passed. So we happily judge the past, in part because we want to understand it, in part because we want to learn from it, and in part because we may be surprised or even incredulous at what we individually or collectively did yesterday, or years ago.

When you think about it, though, it becomes increasingly clear that yesterday, in the past, we *did not have* today's ethics, morals, standards, insights, and understanding. Accordingly, it becomes increasingly clear that we *cannot* judge yesterday with today's yardsticks. It makes no logical sense—and yet, we love to do it.

From speakers on campus with questionable opinions to Michael Jackson, we use today's yardsticks to judge people, often *in their entirety,* by *certain aspects* of their history. We also love to *speculate* about a different past and use today's popular values to *modify* history. "Had I not said or done XYZ back then, what would the other person have said or done?" Or "If they didn't commit those heinous acts, I'd like their art much better." We seem to love reinventing the past, and if we can't, we are often quick to condemn what we, today, don't approve of *in the past.* This is silly.

> Speculating about a different past is about as futile as judging it from today's vantage points.

Why such black-and-white approaches to flawed humans? Many historical figures did great things *and* terrible things— shocking! Where did we get the idea that those we admire aren't allowed to be flawed? Aren't we, today, also all flawed, with skeletons in the closet, with shortcomings and failings? Will *parts of us* one day also be judged with yet-unknown future standards? Would our current-day achievements then possibly be eliminated from the future's historical look backward—because we're complex, flawed, and human? Who came up with the idea that *today's* artists and auteurs aren't—or shouldn't be—as complex and flawed as those of the past? This is all very silly.

> An unrealistic *all-or-nothing* view
> of being human benefits no one.

So what does that leave us? Fundamentally, this only leaves us *one* thing, and that is to *accept history* as the only possible choice—*back then.* Now then, if we want to, we could do things differently today and going forward. The past in no way whatsoever can be changed: that was then, and this is now. The *judging* of the past is not even possible—in fact, it's a conceptual error. We, who we are today, weren't there. Judging the past from today's vantage point at best creates a state of cognitive dissonance within us. At worst, it punishes us for being human.

> The only sensible thing to do with history
> is to accept it.

What this entails in part is the deep recognition and acceptance that it's *okay to let go of decisions made by anybody in the past.* Many of us refuse to accept parts of our individual or collective past, and by doing so, we artificially limit our responsibility and our ability to learn from history. There is no other option besides accepting history just as it transpired, warts and all. If there was another option, we'd take it. But there is none.

> Righteous indignation is not a virtue.

Furthermore, *learning* from the past becomes a lot easier and more helpful if we *don't* judge it before we attempt to understand it. Our quick judgment *will* cloud our understanding, and not in helpful ways. The best way to understand the past and learn from it is to accept it exactly as it transpired, with all the good and bad, *then* try to understand it, and *then* maybe, if we're able to, learn lessons that will inform our behavior today and going forward. Tall order, yes. Impossible order, no. Reasonable, yes. Better options, no.

> Judgment of the past clouds our ability
> to see it as it was—and understand it.

Suspending judgment is incredibly hard to do. It requires a ton of mental discipline and astute self-awareness, as you'll have to check yourself to see if you're able to look at something without making snap judgments about it. Yet, once we realize that this *looking at the past without judgment* is instrumental in understanding it, and therefore instrumental in learning from it—then it becomes a lot more compelling to suspend judgment when looking at the past.

> If we don't understand the past,
> we are prone to repeat it.

Try to practice looking at your individual past and our collective histories without judgment, even if just for a moment. It's okay to let go of decisions made in the past. Try to acknowledge complexities, contradictions, and flaws. Realize that we cannot understand everything and that we never know how others got to where they have gone. See if that changes your ability to understand and learn. There is much relief and freedom in fully realizing that we simply cannot—and therefore ought not to—judge anything behind us with today's yardsticks. It's a trap to do so—see how much you can free yourself from doing so. That was then, this is now, and the *then* is best not conflated with the *now*.

# OUR (UNREALISTIC) EXPECTATIONS OF OTHERS

This happens to all of us: someone we interact with behaves outside of the norm, or outside of our expectations, and we are surprised and possibly taken aback. And then it happens again. And again. Lo and behold, almost all of us are continually surprised, as if each time is the first time. This is weird.

It seems as if we continue to use the typical societal standards to reset our expectations for that person's behavior even *after* those expectations have proven to be untrue. In general, past behavior is the best predictor of future behavior. Yet, we just don't use *that* person's past behavior to set the standard for *that* person's future behavior!

*Expectations are only helpful*
*as long as they turn out to be accurate.*

It's been said that insanity is doing the same thing over and over again and expecting different results. If that's the case, then most of us may be insane ;-) So often, we simply don't adjust our expectations when the world acts and responds in ways we truly could anticipate. Not only do we not adjust our expectations, but we often feel frustrated when someone doesn't comply with our expectations, and we then feel the desire to express that in some form. One way to do that is as incredulity: "How can they be that way?" Shockingly, people *are* the way they are—and we could have known better. In fact, if we wanted to be incredulous, it might be more appropriate to direct that sentiment at ourselves!

*Assuming things is hardly ever a good idea.*

While it can serve us at times to rely on automatic assumptions (e.g., when navigating traffic), it does not serve us in relationships. Take a step back, breathe, and allow the other person the freedom to be *just the way they are today*. Doing this, we might learn more about one another and have the opportunity to become less judgmental friends, lovers, or partners. And who wouldn't want that.

> Check out your expectations of others
> and adjust them based on reality.

We ourselves might appreciate not feeling boxed into the expectations of others. Take a step back and relax your expectations—and update them when they've been corrected by the behavior of others. Others will love you for it, and you'll be more successful in your own relationships.

Wishing for others to be different from how and who they are is tempting but unreasonable. Turn the tables in your mind and see if *you'd* like it if others wished you were different from how and who you are! If you'd like to be accepted just the way you are, the first step in that direction is your accepting *others* just the way they are—maybe especially if their behavior doesn't jibe with your expectations.

> Wishful thinking means
> you're not paying attention.

Be clear, get clear, and act with the eye-opening sobriety that presents itself when wishful thinking takes a back seat. Discover others anew and give them the chance to surprise you. Accept them as they are, for only then will they accept you the way you are. And wouldn't we all like that!?

# HELPING—WHO DOES IT HELP?

elping others enjoys a fantastic reputation. Who doesn't like a noble helper who empathetically alleviates suffering? Society rewards helpers more than almost anybody else. Many helpers are helpers because it in part defines who they are. They are people who focus on others *before* they focus on themselves. On the surface, we process that as altruism, being kind, giving, and selfless. But we usually forget to look at *why* the helper seems so selfless and *whom* the helping is really working for. Often, "helping" is a fast way for the helper to feel one up. We may not consider this consciously, but when helping a "weaker" person, most of us feel stronger and better. And the plot thickens.

Being a helper means being selfless.
Or does it?

One of the great "benefits" of being a helper is that it allows us to not focus on ourselves. We get to focus on someone else's misery, misfortune, pain, or feelings of threat. As such helpers, we may personally feel weakened or threatened precisely when we're dredging up our helper identity. Wait, what!? We might help others simply in order to meet our own needs, or at least to avoid dealing with our own demons for the time being. If we focus on someone else's threats, our own threats can recede into the background for a while.

Helping others with that background story of our own may mean that we end up not helping others at all. If our helping is mainly serving our own needs, we won't even notice when the weaker person no longer needs our help.

It feels so good to be the competent helper that we may overshoot our stated goal by a mile. Helping in this way primarily works for the helper, and helping can be their drug of choice. When helping feels so good, we can overlook the true impact of our helping, on both ourselves and the people we appear to help. It can serve as a massive distraction for all involved.

Helping can be an addiction.

If we're addicted to helping, chances are we'll start managing the emotions of those we help, and we do this primarily because we're unwilling or unable to manage our own emotions. "Professional" helpers abandon their own self-work and, instead of paying the price for it, end up basking in the light of the selfless helper. Such helpers forgo dealing with their own shadows, their own demons, their own anxiety, and their own threats. Having abandoned themselves, they focus on the weaker people around them, and they thrive on *being of service* to those in (apparently) greater need. While this *appears* to be noble, quite often it's the helpers who are in greater need themselves.

Such helping doesn't serve those in need of help as well as it could and maybe should. "Selfless helpers" often end up helping beyond what's healthy for those in need, and often project their own needs and past experiences onto those that are being helped. Such helpers often project their own pain on others. When we see others in situations that were threatening for *us* before, we often rev up and project our own fears and imaginations on others. We may "help" others with things they actually need no help with at all. We may in fact make things worse. And not help ourselves because we divert energy and attention from our own insecurities and needs.

Inappropriate helping can make things worse.

We can dress this up as empathy, altruism, selflessness, and just all-around human goodness; however, we may be mistaken and misguided. Our own imaginations about serving others are *not* reliable yardsticks toward the greater good. While it's natural to want to help those in pain, we may teach them how to get rewards for demonstrating suffering. We may foster and increase dependence in them, and our great assistance may be overwhelming enough for them that they'll lose the sense of when our help has been enough. And who hasn't been in the uncomfortable position of having to tell a "helper" that it's good now and that they can please stop helping us now!? It's hard to tell a helper off. "Professional helpers" may know this secret unconsciously!

Being a helper is such a compelling identity!

If we are addicted to helping, we'll find a way to make it sound good to ourselves. We'll convince ourselves first, and then we'll convince the rest of the world with our apparently selfless actions *how great we are.* Chances are, we *only* need all this convincing and conniving because we don't feel so great about ourselves in the first place. We may cover this up with the help of grandiose means. We may even tell those we help how strong they are, and while helping, we'll shower them with compliments. I mean, who has the wherewithal to turn down a compliment while suffering!?

Needing to feel one up generally comes from a fundamental state of feeling one down in general. This may have happened during our childhood, during college, or at our job. We've taken a hit. Shit happens. But if it's our shit, we ought to deal with it ourselves and do the self-work that it'll take before we develop a "helping" identity or launch into "helping" professions. While it sounds trite, it's rather true that you need to help yourself before you're fit to help others. Self-work rules, and besides, in the end you can't work on anybody else but *yourself.* We generally don't have the mandate from others to work on them. It's often overreaching.

Help yourself before you decide to help others.

If you are using "helping" as a substitute for relieving your own anxieties, take steps back and begin the necessary process of taking responsibility for your own emotions. This is not easy, but it's the healthy way. Only once you've developed good boundaries and a solid sense of self would it be prudent to start helping others substantially. Being a helper, privately or professionally, can be great—but check with yourself if you're doing it for reasons of your own or because someone around you truly needs help and has asked for your help. It makes a world of difference.

# AUTHENTICITY VS. MAKING SHIT UP

When was the last time you met someone who didn't feel inadequate in some respect? It's practically a pandemic—almost all of us suffer from not being enough, or too much. Since this sucks and is hard to admit to, most of us pretend we have our shit together and that we know what we're doing. Mostly, neither is true. And after doing this for many years, most of us find this *impression management* game tiring. It is. Pretending takes a lot of energy.

In some ways it's normal that we all walk through life being busy managing the impressions we want to give. We feel we have something to lose if we don't manage how we're being perceived. For most of us, this actually is a lot of work. But life's complicated enough without having to remember made-up stuff. And of course we sometimes forget that we can only manage *ourselves* and we inadvertently start managing *others*. This is of course a no-go, and fails with great reliability. Yet again, most of us do it.

We all know intellectually that it's a hell of a lot easier to simply be authentic and truthful, even about our own perceived inadequacies. And eventually most people *will* see through our managed identities and dressed-up truths and stumble upon our apparent weak spots, physical and psychological blemishes, and incongruences. Everybody knows that it's usually just a matter of time. What's fascinating about this is that our own perceived inadequacies are only unacceptable to *us*.

Our inadequacies are only unacceptable to *us*.

This can be hard to believe, but becomes self-evident when you simply try it out. As an experiment, introduce some simple and bare authenticity to someone, and see how they respond. Amazingly, others are a lot more forgiving of us than we ourselves are! This holds true even about our darker secrets, our deeply guarded flaws, the things we imagine would prompt others to reject us. Shockingly, they do no such thing, but instead feel *closer* to us! What!?

Making up shit and keeping others in the dark makes us *and others* work unnecessarily hard, and lowers trust all around. And others can feel let down when they eventually find out about what we consider our inadequacies *if* we've pretended those flaws don't exist. As long as we share them with owned vulnerability *when the time is right*, it turns out that others are rather accepting of our foibles.

There's a cost to us and to those around us when we aren't authentic, hiding our inadequacies and engaging in impression management. But the biggest cost is the effect this has on *our own* psyche. Trapping ourselves into rigid ideas of how we *should be* is one of the most reliable pathways to depression. It keeps us from developing a healthy awareness of who we truly are. Yes, we can always strive to improve ourselves, but we can like, rather than dislike, ourselves enough to even want to do that.

On the upside, authenticity is what actually comes naturally to us—it's what happens *before* we start hiding and managing information about us. It's easier and more effective to not tell little white lies—both to ourselves and to others. It's also hard to know when a little lie turns into a big lie, because, let's face it, most of us are biased in our favor. And managing impressions can be a lot of work, as we have to remember what we told whom and when and where. Making shit up is tiring.

The big secret about authenticity is that it's fundamentally lovable.

Maybe the biggest secret about authenticity, though, is that it's fundamentally lovable. It's like magic—try it. Try being 100% authentic about something with someone and see how they react. They may not only feel closer to you, but they may also be more forgiving—and they will be drawn to you, even admire you. Authenticity is fundamentally lovable. Once you know this and have had some experience of it, it becomes a relief to no longer manage how we're being perceived, and instead simply be authentic. And plain honest. Less to remember, less to manage, less to make up. In the end, it's just easier for everybody. Authenticity truly is fundamentally lovable. It's like magic! Give it a whirl.

# OUR OWN CHALLENGING EMOTIONS

It's not easy to know where our challenging emotions come from, what they mean, and how to process and handle them in constructive ways. We often find ourselves stuck in repetitive loops of thoughts and feelings which keep us from feeling free, being clear, and moving forward constructively. We can be our own worst enemy when it comes to successfully handling our own emotional wildlife. Here are some constructive ways of dealing with our emotions that free us from being held hostage by our less-than-helpful thoughts and emotions.

# CONSCIENCE IS THE ORGAN OF BELONGING

Most of us believe that we have a good conscience when we do good things and a bad conscience when we do bad things. This sounds true, but it's not accurate. Our conscience is much more complex than that. One only needs to look at the Holocaust to quickly understand that terrible things have been done with apparent good conscience by millions—who apparently just followed orders, and did so with, from what we understand, surprising good conscience.

Unimaginable atrocities have been committed with good conscience.

And one only needs to look to the countless victims of partner or domestic abuse in order to understand that good things—such as an abuse victim seeking help or getting out—have often been done with a bad conscience. Many times, abuse victims even report a bad conscience when simply entertaining the good or healthy action, and they report that a bad conscience kept them from doing what would have been right by *them*. Even those of us who haven't been in abusive situations can realize that we've sometimes done the right thing with a bad conscience—and maybe, at times, *not* done the right thing with an apparent good conscience.

A good conscience has little to do with doing apparent good, and a bad conscience has little to do with doing apparent bad.

So what does that tell us? The big revelation about conscience is that, in a nutshell, it functions as our *organ of belonging.* What does that mean? Not unlike we use our nose to discern pleasurable smells from noxious odors, our ears to discern pleasurable sounds from alarming noises—we use our conscience to discern which behavior ensures inclusion to our social group and which behaviors may get us kicked out. As such, conscience is as critical a tool or organ as are our sense of smell or our hearing. So how does our conscience, our *organ of belonging,* operate and help us survive?

We do things with a good conscience when we believe or trust, consciously or unconsciously, that our actions ensure belonging to our group or tribe, thereby providing us with a sense of safety and identity. This group or tribe may be our family of origin, our group of peers, our nation, our current family, our circle of friends—or our adopted tribe, such as a gang, a religious group, or a political movement. Belonging to any of these groups or tribes makes us feel good. It is because of these "good" feelings that it's critical to be aware that while doing things that apparently ensure our inclusion, we may commit terrible acts without feeling bad at all.

Conscience is the human organ of belonging.

And when we unconsciously or consciously believe, or fear, that our behaviors or actions will threaten our sense of inclusion and belonging, we may do them with a bad conscience or not do them at all—no matter how "right" or healthy or "good" those actions might be for us. We will often sacrifice ourselves in order to *not* jeopardize our sense of belonging, safety, and identity. This may mean staying with an abusive partner, capitulating to social or peer pressure, partaking in hazing at college, or simply not speaking up for what we believe, when we assume that the majority appears to be against our contemplated stance. Again, it's critical to be aware that if it threatens our sense of inclusion or acceptance, we may not do the right, good, ethical, or healthy thing. And if we reluctantly *do* do it, we may do it with a bad conscience.

In addition to our general sense of conscience, there's also one's *personal moral code*—what one deeply and unwaveringly believes to be right or wrong regardless of affinity to any group. This may sound mushy, but following such deep personal moral code "just feels right," and betraying it "just feels wrong," and very deeply so. Because of the depth of such personal moral code, *not* following it, or not *being able* to follow it, can result in what's often referred to as *moral injury*.

> Moral Injury is when your
> personal code is at war with *you*.

Moral injury is the kind of suffering one can experience in high-stakes situations when things go seriously sideways. Such derailments can have harmful results that challenge deeply held personal moral convictions and affect our ability to trust ourselves—and others—in the future. What triggers such harm and loss of trust in ourselves and in others may be something we *did*, something we *didn't* do but believe we *should* have done, something we *witnessed*, or something that was *done to us*. Betraying—or being forced to betray—your personal moral code can lead to profound internal suffering. This may mean a deep loss of trust in ourselves and others, or feeling guilt, shame, self-condemnation, outrage, despair, and even suicidality.

Moral injury predominantly affects military veterans, but it can also affect survivors of sexual assault and abuse, imprisoned people, doctors, nurses, and law enforcement personnel in extreme conditions, and even Alzheimer's caregivers or veterinarians. *Moral injury* is no joke—it makes us the walking wounded, and it's paramount that we don't ignore it in ourselves or those around us who may be afflicted by it.

# OWNING YOUR EXPERIENCE

"*You know how you feel when someone you're close to dies—you get so sad.*" The vast majority of us talk like that when we're talking about *our* experience, our emotions. Or we might say something like, "*You know, he was so loved, everybody's so sad.*" For some reason, we've collectively adopted a conversational style that allows us to outsource our own subjective emotional experience. While we may do this to build possible rapport and solicit empathy, it's curious that we choose to do so by apparently not talking about *ourselves* at all, but instead talking about *others*—usually the collective "*you.*"

What does speaking about oneself in "you" or "we" terms do to our own experience? And what does it do to the listener? Try saying the italicized first sentence and see how you feel after saying it. Then, compare that feeling to how you feel after saying, instead, *"I was close to her, and I am so sad she died."* Almost all the time, speaking in "I" terms—or *owning* the experience—makes us *feel more* by identifying more with what we've just said. So if *owning* our experience means we'll feel more of it, we're *also* more likely to feel more responsibility for our feelings, but we actually often don't want that! When it comes to our difficult emotions, we often don't know how to speak about them in authentic ways. So we may rope our listeners into the "you" equation to share the burden and make it easier for us.

It feels harder to own negative experiences than it does to own positive experiences.

This doesn't hold so true for our *positive* emotions! Most of us (for example, when winning a competition) don't externalize our experience—we don't say, *"You know how you feel when you've won a competition you've worked hard for."* In those (positive) instances we're more inclined to truly speak about ourselves, *own our experience,* and instead say things like, *"I feel so great about winning this competition after having worked so hard for it."* Positive experiences are much easier to *own.* We feel the power of the positive experience and have little trouble owning it.

How does this all play out for the listener? Speakers who talk about themselves to us in *you* terms in some fashion *rely on us* to relate to their experience, usually to agree or to provide validation or support. But we may or may not have had the experience we're being told about, and thus we may or may not know how it feels for the speaker. That makes the validation process hit and miss. Besides, most of us don't enjoy being roped into someone else's emotional drama.

It's incredibly powerful
to fully own one's experience.

However, the *biggest* downside to speaking about one's experiences in "you" or "we" language is that it makes our experience something others can *argue* with. *Arguing with someone's experience* is something many of us do, and many of us have experienced *ourselves* when others have argued with our own experience—and none of it is helpful to anybody. In fact, it can be infuriating and even devastating when others take issue with our own experience. If, however, I report my experience in "I" terms, speaking authentically about how **I** feel, then nobody can take issue with it and argue with it. This may sound simple, but owning your experience has profound and liberating effects, especially in intimate relationships, where arguing with someone's experience takes place the most.

Another unfortunate way for others to *argue with our experience* presents itself when we state our *subjective* experience in *objective* terms. If someone says, "*It's cold in here,*" the listener may not *hear* what you're actually saying (that you're cold), and will often *take issue* with your statement. If your listener doesn't feel cold, they often will respond by saying, "*I don't think it's cold in here*"—thereby missing the entire point of your statement, which was to report that you're cold. So instead of a blanket (to warm you), you will likely get an argument (about the room temperature)!

Nobody can take your owned experience away from you.

Most of us have been there, and most of us find it terribly frustrating to have our experience argued with. As it turns out, we can do something *quite simple* that will make it nearly impossible for others to argue with our experience. If we use "I" instead of "you," "we," or "they," and if we don't share apparently objective statements (such as "it's cold in here"), we become more of who we are—true and authentic individuals with a perspective that is uniquely ours. And nobody can argue with that. It can be a tremendous relief. Try it sometime.

We've all gotten so used to having our experience argued with that we may have forgotten how it feels when we own our experience, moment by moment. Starting to *own* your experience can be difficult and challenging, and you may try it a little here and there to see how it goes. But any challenges are far outweighed by the immense positive effects of speaking only about yourself, reporting your experience authentically, and owning your emotions. We may be positively surprised by how impossible it is for others to argue with our authentic reporting of our experience!

Owning your experience creates safety and is critical to your mental health.

Trying this in one-to-one relationships may be a little challenging. Trying it in groups may be even more challenging. We don't want to rock the boat or be the odd man out, and we often even look to others to see if anybody shares our experience *before* expressing it. Isn't that interesting!? We often don't want to be alone with our experience, and we often don't want to feel responsible for upsetting the status quo. Yet, even in group settings, it turns out to be surprisingly doable to simply report your own experience. You may even serve as a role model for others to open up authentically about their experience. All in all, speaking authentically about your own experience, and owning it, ends up being a win-win.

Owning your experience is an act of self-love.

# SELF-DOUBT—YOUR WORST ENEMY

Nobody has ever died saying, "I wish I'd had more self-doubt." For most of our life, we walk around with plenty of self-doubt, and for some reason we apparently believe that this is a good idea—otherwise, why do it? In fact, it seems so good an idea that we just won't give up on it! Then, later in life—if we're lucky—we realize that all those years of self-doubt were for nothing. Nothing at all. Wasted negative self-talk, critical and unrelenting conversations with ourselves that simply held us back.

It's easy to project onto those who seem very self-confident: we're sure *they* don't have self-doubts *the way we do*. Boy, are we wrong. *Everybody* has them, those at the top and those at the bottom. People with apparently great self-confidence are not immune to self-doubt at all. It's practically a pandemic with no vaccine.

The messages to support our self-doubt are everywhere. Parents more often than not behaved in ways that gave us the sense that there was something wrong with us (which we have since internalized), the advertising industry shows people better-looking and better-off than us, partners of choice may criticize us, organized religion may chastise us (or we *feel* criticized by it), and even strangers may look at us weirdly. There are near limitless avenues of encouragement toward second-guessing oneself and negative self-talk. Self-doubt is perhaps one of the most insidious afflictions of modern life.

---

Be skeptical of your thoughts. Just because you have them doesn't make them true.

---

We internalize real or imagined criticism and negativity and *appropriate* the real or imagined voices of others and make them *our* internal voices. And then the beating up on ourselves begins, a vicious cycle that goes down, down, and further down. It's a terrible treadmill to be on, and a very difficult one to get off of. Curing ourselves of self-doubt, negative self-talk—and self-hate—is *not* easy. However, it *is* doable, and that's really fantastic news.

Undoing many years of poor and unhelpful programming in the self-worth department is arduous work, and it requires professional assistance in order to add an impartial and trained perspective. But it's good work, and well worth it—if for no other reason than that others will find it hard to love us if we don't love ourselves. So in order to allow the love of others in, it's a good idea to tear down as many obstacles as possible that are in the way—in the way of love. Self-doubt and self-hate *are* obstacles.

Doubt can be healthy.
Self-doubt hardly ever is.

To cut down on the time it takes to overcome self-doubt, take some time with these pointed questions:

- How much time have you invested into self-doubt in your life up to now?

- How well has self-doubt paid off in the past?

- How many more days, months, and years will you allow yourself to be plagued by self-doubt?

- Have you ever tried to love someone who's full of self-doubt and self-hate? It's hard, if not impossible. Would you like to be lovable?

- What if the only thing that stood in your way was your own conversation with yourself?

How well has self-doubt paid off in the past?

Generally, there are no shortcuts in life. But it's possible to look deep into the silliness of an unhelpful dynamic and make radical choices. What if next time you feel that all too familiar voice of self-doubt coming on, you short-circuit its old pattern and simply *do the opposite of what that voice keeps you from doing?* It's *possible*, right? It *can* be done!

Since most of our negative self-talk is relatively unconscious, you only have to short-circuit that old pattern a few times in order to kick the unconscious habit of self-doubt upstairs into your *consciousness,* your *awareness.* Once it's in your awareness, it will have a much harder time keeping you in its grasp, because you're now on to it and its plot to hold you back, and you can even have conversations with those parts of yourself that used to self-sabotage you.

Listening to your inner critic means taking
advice from someone who doesn't like you.

Every time that silly, unloving voice reports to duty again,
you now have *practice*—and an increasing number of
events where you did the opposite of what you cautioned
yourself not to do—and you're *still alive*. Try this and see
just how *possible* it can be to evict self-doubt and self-hate
from where it's been living rent-free for far too long: inside
your fine brain, body, heart, and soul.

Imagine how it would be to go through the day without
doubting or second-guessing yourself. Sure, you'll make
some mistakes, and you'll learn from them and adapt—but
that's entirely different from *not* doing things and then *not*
learning from that. You can do what it takes to kick self-
doubt to the curb. It's a major drag to live with it, and we've
all gotten used to it to the point of no longer remembering

how unhelpful it is. Most of us believe that "this and that is wrong with me" is a natural state. It is not.

And if you believe that your inner critic and voices of self-doubt accurately reflect how the world feels toward you, well, remember that you're listening to someone who doesn't like you! As it turns out, others are *always* much more accepting of our perceived inadequacies than we are—always. Few are as unforgiving of us as we ourselves are. Nobody is more critical of us than we are. This is insane.

Try taking a break from self-doubt and your inner critic. You can always resume beating yourself up if being accepting and loving toward yourself turns out to have been a mistake. And if you said or did something and then look back at it critically, remember that it's not for you to decide how good you were. In fact, what you think is irrelevant, since you didn't do it for yourself in the first place. All the energy invested into evaluating your *past* self is a giant waste of time. If others say what you said or did was good, then you did well. All you can do is love yourself, prepare, and show up.

# REACTIVITY VS. SPACIOUSNESS

I n an era of ever-shortening attention spans and pervasive diagnoses such as ADHD, where longhand may be a thing of the past and where sound bites have replaced stories, we find ourselves *responding* more than initiating, *reacting* more than acting, and *escaping* the flood of information rather than seeking to fill our buckets of thirst for information, stimulation, and satiation in gentle, careful, and thought-out ways.

To many of us, the past often appears to have been better. While this is always debatable, clocks don't turn backward, and novel phenomena are usually here to stay. It's no secret that *reactivity* is up in general and that most of us have, as a result, become *less spacious in our thinking and feeling.* We perceive that there's *less* time to answer, to respond, to share, but also seemingly less time to explore what and how we think and feel about things. We only have so much capacity to process information, mental or emotional, and that bandwidth gets taken up with, well, what we allow in, and most of us allow a lot in.

In simple social conversations, it's easy to observe levels of mental disorganization, avoidance of topics, short attention spans, emotional reactivity, talking out loud to think, and liking to hear oneself think and talk. Often, our conversational partners respond to us by going off on tangents, arguing circumstantially, being indirect, focusing on the edges and not on the center. Their thinking is often neither linear nor clear, and they often talk around and around what may be simple issues. Associations they make can be incredibly loose, accuracy of hearing can be very low, and people often make amazing deductions based on woefully little information. Or they just plain check out. "*What did you say?*"

When dynamics such as these happen, our bars get lowered—our yardstick for what passes for a "good conversation" changes, and it's easy to forget that there are alternative ways of handling one's thoughts and feelings. *Spacious* thinking and *spacious* feeling means *lowering the level of reactivity*. Pausing. Waiting until the other party is finished. Listening carefully. Reflecting first, before interrupting or disagreeing. To see what one feels before one acts on it. To maybe even *think* about one's feelings before sharing them with someone else. To maybe even explore your own thinking to see if it makes sense and contributes value.

> Spaciousness is required
> to access your intuition.

Spaciousness, whether mental or emotional, introduces the p a u s e s we all need in order to *digest* what has just happened. While it's most commonly believed that communication happens while we speak or listen, its most important part happens when we *don't* speak—in the pauses where our listeners can "swallow" and digest the information we've just shared. If someone speaks at us without any pause, most of it will go right past us. We *need* those pauses in order to absorb the input. Otherwise there is no chance for successful communication.

In an era of near-constant input, it becomes increasingly hard to afford the pauses, the times where *nothing* happens. It becomes harder and harder to find the spaces in-between things, to claim the pauses we must have in order to absorb, digest, and make sense of what we've heard or seen or felt. Finding such spaces, such spaciousness, becomes increasingly necessary in order to *not* stay in a constant state of overwhelm—and ensuing reactivity. It may be no surprise that movements around well-being, mindful living, and meditation have all gained mainstream momentum in recent times.

Mental and emotional spaciousness
help us separate what we need and want
from what we don't need and don't want.

Few adults will argue that our conversations, interactions, and our well-being would benefit from less speed, less reactivity, and more calmness. Mental and emotional spaciousness *is* about such calmness. It's about an inner state of pausing, *s l o w i n g* things down, taking time, making time, and getting off the hamster wheel of whatever it is that "has to happen right now." This can start with little steps such as responding to someone's statement or question with "I'm going to think about this." Or responding to an email after sitting on it for a day. Or just thinking about your response before you offer it. Or reducing your contribution to its most important essence. Or participating in conversations with less interrupting. Maybe simply try to pay attention to your breathing whenever you feel the urge to interrupt.

Uncluttering your mind and heart makes room
for what you want in your mind and heart.

New worlds will open up if you decrease your reactivity and increase your spaciousness. Affording yourself emotional and mental breathing space will make you a calmer, more considerate, and more resilient person. It will increase your presence, and by that, your power. It will make others seek your company more, as they will feel that you're a good listener and that you manage to remain calm while their head is on fire. And it will show you that you can be yourself with a lot more inner wiggle room and, gasp, inner peace.

# KARMA: WHAT GOES AROUND, COMES AROUND?

The Eastern concept of karma has been adopted in Western popular culture, in that the events which happen *after* a person's actions may be considered *natural consequences* of that person's actions. The idea that the beneficial or harmful effects one has on the world will return to oneself is not new—we've been here before. Many people nowadays will sum this up colloquially with "what goes around comes around." The notions of "good karma" (for "good" actions yielding good stuff down the road) and "bad karma" (for "bad" actions yielding bad stuff down the road) echo through many brains over many years—without much critical examination.

While most Westerners have some knowledge that karma is a Sanskrit word and comes out of Hindu mythology, few understand its origin enough to differentiate its true meaning from the popular modern-day Western use. In Hindu mythology, karma is a somewhat complex dynamic, as the Hindu mentality looks at *time* not as a straight line or even as a river, but as a *circle* in which everything repeats itself and turns back to its own beginnings. Karma in the Hindu sense needs to be understood in that circular context. Western mindsets, religions, and philosophies don't usually share such circular notions.

The Hindu meaning, which is often borrowed by Westerners, *does* entail that there are effects or consequences to one's actions or deeds, which include one's *intent*. Such consequences are understood to influence not only one's future in this life, but also the nature and quality of *future* lives, since karma includes the foundational Hindu belief of rebirth. Western understandings of nature and life do not include beliefs in rebirths.

So how did the notion of karma become so popular in the West—seemingly as a guiding principle toward engaging in good deeds and toward staying away from bad deeds, or at least negatively judged behaviors? Humans abhor a *vacuum of reason*. We ask ourselves questions such as "*Why did this happen to me?*" or "Why is the world so unfair?" or "Why is there so much senseless suffering?" We wonder how "good" people can have such bad luck while "wicked" people can have such good luck. We struggle to *make sense* of many things, and *especially* of tragic events. We wonder if it is all just random coincidence, or if there is some sort of larger *plan* into which inequality, unfairness, and suffering somehow fit. There appear to be no reliable answers. Some of us turn to religion for meaning, and within religion, often to a God.

"My karma ran over your dogma."

The call for a God works somewhat for those who are steeped in personal or organized religiosity. Yet even believers in a

God can find it challenging to understand suffering since they firmly believe that their God is fundamentally benevolent, loving and omnipotent. This, one reasons, should entail God being able to alleviate suffering—yet, he often appears to not do so. And for those who are not disciples of major religious movements, the call for a God doesn't work at all. Since organized Western religion has lost some of its hold on humanity in recent decades, an increasing number of people turn to notions such as karma to make sense of those things that don't appear to make sense.

Having a sense of meaning helps greatly in coping with apparent unfairness and especially with senseless suffering. If we don't *have* meaning, we want to *assign* meaning, and there seems to be some deep need to do so. It's an almost desperate act, like clinging to any floating object when we feel we're drowning. But why such despair? Why do we feel we *have* to ask questions for which there appear no ready answers? Couldn't we just live in bewilderment and astonishment, in awe of ultimate riddles such as the meaning of things, the meaning of life? Apparently not. For some reason, *any* answer seems to trump sheer puzzlement. We don't appear to be able to simply revel in the great mysteries of life—good and bad—without assigning meaning.

The human mind, for reasons we don't understand, just *wants answers!* And we don't want them tomorrow, we want them *today!* But does this urge for instant gratification miss important parts of the picture? What about the idea that meaning is *unknowable?* This is almost preposterous—with our investment in the advancement of science, we somehow aren't willing to tolerate the idea that meaning simply may not be knowable. We want to make sense of things for us as groups and tribes and nations, but especially for us *personally.* "Why me?" presents itself long before we give puzzlement a chance. Karma, then, is a handy tool to make sense of things for *me*—it can't just be that there's no rhyme or reason to what happens to *me.*

Yet, with definitive answers rather completely out of reach, we gladly overlook lots of details even when they don't add up, as is the case with our modern understanding and use of karma. For one, Western popular use of karma neglects the understanding that we all live as part of complex systems—karma views things from an individualistic perspective of simple cause and effect: "Do something good today, and your windfall tomorrow will have been caused by it." We know we are all part of systems, most of which we don't totally understand—and yet, we grasp the first floating object that *appears* to keep us from drowning in a world that just doesn't make sense.

Belief has amazing powers—it can make us "claim" that if something is not fair today or these days or in this life, there *must* be redemption later down the road, even if that means in another life. This is what scientists would call wishful thinking. We conveniently overlook the fact that if redemption is *down the road*, we can't possibly measure its correlation to today's events. But deferring redemption into the future for some reason makes the (often painful) present so much more bearable. Karma, with its borrowed and adapted definition, helps alleviate the apparent unfairness or meaninglessness of life, especially for those who are not steeped in organized religiosity.

This way, our inclination to believe in karma, as an imaginary universal law, serves as a future-retroactive great leveler of all thoughts and deeds. Thus, Western use of karma is not very different from most major organized religions, which also derive their functionality, integrity, and attractiveness from a post-life idea of redemption or damnation. Given that nobody has come "back" to this life or been provably incarnated (Hindu-karma-style) as a human with karmic memory and any acceptable proof whatsoever, it's amazing that we invest our faith in some future time where judgment will be served and the inequalities of today will be leveled out. Banking on things getting leveled out down the road can be an easy way to abdicate responsibility here and now. It can be tempting. If there will be "justice" later, then we can allow ourselves to forgo being "just" right now.

"Karma means I can rest easy at night knowing that all the people I treated badly had it coming." Or does it?

Children believe fanciful things, such as invisible worlds holding magical answers to their developing minds. This is partly because they have not yet gained a conceptual understanding of life and reality as we know it. There and then, magical thinking may well be appropriate. That we as adults blithely subscribe to an afterlife and redemptive notions or down-the-road great leveling dynamics such as karma is creative and inventive. What other nature-defying laws might we collectively dream up?

But what to do if one forgoes kicking the can down the road? How does one handle, process, and digest today's inequalities, unfairness, and apparently senseless suffering? These are big questions. It might help to appreciate that these questions are all based on the assumption that in life there *should* be equality, fairness, and no senseless suffering. Few of us ever question those assumptions. It's interesting to note that *life itself* questions those assumptions for us all on a daily basis. Yet we so rarely take the hint that just maybe life's not supposed to be as fair or pain-free as we'd all like it to be.

# THE ONLY QUESTION WHEN FEELING AGITATED

One of the easiest things ever is to point our fingers at others. We're almost wired to immediately see the fault outside of us when something rubs us the wrong way. It's as if there's an unconscious playbook that reads "we did the right thing—or so it appears—and therefore the reason for having our feathers ruffled *must* be outside of us." And then the blame game begins. Incredulous, we're then almost surprised that the other party doesn't acknowledge their apparent wrongdoing, and when pushback comes, we are likely to dig in and shore up our defensive arguments. We're right, after all.

As it turns out, nobody likes being held responsible for us having our knickers twisted. And when confronted, it likely feels like an attack to them. And when attacked, most of us feel pushed into a corner, and—guess what—we come out fighting. Usually defensive or angry. And it all goes downhill from there, and within seconds or minutes we're in a confrontation with no apparent winner. It's a bona fide shit-show, and we've all been there: so convinced *others* are responsible for how *we* feel. We don't even notice how much power we've just given them and how quickly we've assigned the victim role to ourselves. Sigh.

When we have relationship issues,
we'll often do more of what we did before,
only with more intensity and anxiety.

We can do better. There *is* a way to not play the blame game, to not fall into the trap of victimization, to *not* grant others power over us, and to not have to find ourselves in dreaded confrontations at all. While it takes two or more to create relationships, our own part of the relationship issue is *the only part* we have control over, that we have the power to change. We inconveniently forget that when we're so sure that it's the other person's responsibility. We also inconveniently forget that they haven't given us the authority to work on them!

It's easy to single out *individuals* as the culprit or the designated patient in a relationship. Yet the reality is that we each play a critical part in producing the anxious symptoms that arise in relationships. Each of us, our behaviors, all the symptoms, and everybody's input—together they all create an interdependent system of behavior. What this means is that if one person changes their contribution to that system or its symptoms, the whole system must change. It's like a mobile—if you flick one part, all the other parts *must* change their status quo. It's inevitable—yet it's only possible if *you* change *your* own contribution. Changing someone else's contribution is *their* responsibility—never yours. Therefore, there's only *one* truly helpful question to ask yourself when you feel agitated by something in a relationship: *How did **I** get here?*

---

Curiosity is the antidote to anxiety.

---

What did **I** do, contribute, not do, conveniently forget, force, manipulate, or hold back? *Find* the answers to these questions. Ask yourself more questions: Does this remind me of something I've experienced before? Do I know this feeling intimately already? Have I been here before with this person? With someone else? Do I feel righteous and indignant? Is somebody making an apparently big deal out of nothing? Did I maybe do something—anything—that could have sparked the other party's strong response? How might things look from their perspective? Be curious about yourself and about others.

There's only one question to ask when you feel agitated by something: *How did I get here?*

Asking yourself this—and only this—question will give you the most control, the most power, the most leverage, the most authority, the best possible outcome—and it will make you a much more desirable person to be around. If you ever manage to make this fundamental shift—from looking outside yourself to looking inside yourself when something feels off—you will have made one of the most profound shifts anybody can ever make.

Remember that you cannot—and therefore must not— work on others or manage others. You can only work on yourself and manage yourself. Remind yourself of those boundaries as you learn to always ask yourself only one question when things aren't going your way: *How did I get here?*

# CONFUSING GUILT AND SHAME

So often, and so easily, we confuse *guilt* with *shame*. We just feel bad about something that happened to us, or because of us, or that we did or did not do, but should or shouldn't have done. It can seem unclear just what we feel so wretched about or why we feel tormented. Most times, we carry that disconcerting past feeling into the present and feel bad *now*. And most often we keep that troubling feeling to ourselves.

When this taxing feeling stays hidden, we might not realize that we have options: we could turn on the light and begin the relief process by first discovering if we feel *guilt* or *shame*. While they are related, they are distinct dynamics. It's critical to separate the two and identify what it is you're actually feeling. If you keep it a secret from others and maybe even from yourself, you'll suffer unnecessarily.

> The big insight about guilt and shame is that
> feeling *guilt* means we *did* something bad,
> feeling *shame* means we feel we *are* bad.

*Guilt* means that we are a good person but did something bad—likely something that jeopardizes our sense of belonging, that violates our own ethics or those of the people we want to belong to. We *did*—or *didn't do*—something that our code dictated we should or should not have done. Accordingly, feelings of guilt can be healthy as they steer us toward a healthy sense of belonging to our people or group of choice. They are like guardrails that keep our behavior from going off the road.

The great news about feeling guilty is that we can remedy it through *insight* and *demonstrated actions of reconciliation* such as *acknowledging wrongdoing, expressing contrition,* and *making amends with those who felt harmed*—and that is fantastic news. Feelings of guilt can be fully overcome. Our sense of belonging can be fully repaired. Gain the insight, acknowledge your "wrongdoing" with contrition, share that with the other party, and propose actions that might lead toward reconciliation. You may also ask what the other party might need in order to be made whole again. It's good stuff all around.

> Guilt is usually anxiety about a projected disapproving response from an *individual person* we want to belong with.

If you have fallen out of touch over something that you feel some guilt about, it's on you to approach the other party. Forget the pleasantries and instead share your process of contrition and take full—100%—responsibility for how you screwed up, with no ifs and buts. Don't seduce yourself into addressing how the other party may have screwed up as well—that would be *their* job. Take a stance of explicit humility and expect nothing in return. Don't overdo it with a lengthy essay. Keep it concise, tight, and clear. As a general rule, your authentic efforts of demonstrated contrition *will be* rewarded.

---

*While guilt causes us to focus on the negative feelings of* others, *shame causes us to focus on our* own *negative feelings.*

---

*Shame,* on the other hand, means that we feel we *are* bad. Something happened to us, or we partook in something that hit us so deep and hard that in the depth of our hearts and minds we've quietly concluded that our true self is defective and flawed. We have feelings of failure and self-contempt, which can easily become toxic and lead to anxiety or depression. If this sense of deep shame stays unaddressed, it can be crippling, feel hopeless, shut us down, and keep us from having healthy relationships. Worst of all, shame makes us feel our punishment is somehow warranted. This sort of shame is not healthy in any way.

We will much more readily admit guilt than shame. Guilt means we *did* screw up, while shame means we *are* screwed up. There's even shame about shame and humiliation about shame, which makes us feel isolated and alone in a complete sense. We may not want to look others in the eye, and in some fashion, we want to disappear. Once we've been shamed and have internalized that shame, we can become convinced that we can never change or recover.

> Shame is usually anxiety about a projected disapproving response by a *group or system* we want to belong to.

Judging, blaming, and shaming is very easy to do, but the consequences can be devastating. This is especially true when we've experienced being shamed *as children*. Many of us might remember being told things like "you are a bad boy or girl." Subconsciously, we *don't* forget those events—

instead, we internalize them and develop deep-seated beliefs that we are, indeed, *bad*. Thus, much deep shame originates from our childhoods. As children, we didn't yet have the conceptual capacity to differentiate between *being fundamentally good* and maybe having *done* something bad—and actually *being* bad.

> If you feel shame, know this:
> you are a *good* person with *faulty* beliefs
> which you can change.

The good news about feeling shame is that there *are* ways to emerge from the darkness it casts upon us. We *can* heal. Find a friend you can trust, maybe a professional, and begin to talk about it. Through talking it out of the dark, and shining light onto the dark, the veil of shame can lift and slowly reduce distress as you free yourself of this toxic *mistaken* identity. It's not simple or easy, but it's possible—

through introspection and therapeutic work on your own or with a professional.

Imagine a life without profound guilt or deep-seated shame! To belong healthily and to love yourself and no longer identify as "defective." It's well worth putting in the effort to rectify what you feel guilty about or doing the hard work to eventually leave your shame-based identity behind you and be lighter, healthier, more connected and happier.

The wonderful thing about guilt and shame is that they both only exist in your mind, meaning they are *all yours* to work through and break free from their emotional hold.

# SEX AND SHAME ARE
# TERRIBLE BEDFELLOWS

Oh, how much shame we all have around sex. It's one of the most natural and compelling drives we know, and yet we shroud it in stigma, taboos, darkness, and shame. We don't do that with our other drives such as eating, drinking, breathing, or sleeping! None of us would be here without sex, all of us want it sometime, most of us enjoy it, and yet, we move it into darkness. We so often treat sex as if it doesn't belong to us, or we to it. This is doing a disservice to our humanity, and to truth. Who's ever been served by having shame around sex? It's not fair, let alone healthy.

All of us have sexual shame; you're not special!

Everybody has issues around sex. Yet sex is as normal as breathing, eating, walking, and sleeping. If we treat it as such and take it out of the closet, which can be done in respectful ways, others will learn something good and healthy, and appreciate you for it. You will be doing yourself, your partner, and those you talk to a service by destigmatizing something that's been in the dark for too long. *Don't* leave your issues around sex in the closet, and don't support your partner in keeping theirs in the closet. Life is not to be lived in closets!

Sex is good for you, shame is not.

Authenticity is sexy and lovable. Be honest. Don't let others guess what you like and want, what you don't like and don't want. Be direct, and others will learn from you. Once you've tried being up-front and direct and honest, you'll find that it can happen remarkably easily. You might even wonder why others are not doing the same thing you've just done.

A little secret about sex and shame is that everybody likes the former and hates the latter. Most of us are freaked out about these terrible bedfellows. Shame has played, and is playing, a number on all of us. It's so much healthier—and more fun—to freak out together: bring it up with friends and partners, make the implicit explicit, and verbalize the things that seem so hard to spell out. Your partner will almost certainly appreciate your example and take a cue from you.

Shame can affect your libido, your boundaries, and your emotional, mental, and physical well-being. Outside of public decency, there's just about nothing good about shame in the sexual realm. Do your very best to ban shame from the bedroom, from your sexual thoughts and sexual feelings. Invite those close to you to be open and explicit about it as well. Make it a conversation you can have, rather than one that should be avoided. Others will appreciate your respectful openness about sex.

# PAIN & SUFFERING, PRESSURE & STRESS

We've all suffered from pain, and we've all gotten stressed out when there's been too much pressure. Many of us live entirely stressful lives, and some of us suffer a lot from either emotional or physical pain. To most of us, pain and suffering are blurred sensations, as are pressure and stress. Of course, it would seem, one does suffer when it hurts and one does get stressed out when the pressure is on. These dynamics are blurred enough that we no longer differentiate between pain and suffering, or between pressure and stress. We just suffer, and we're just stressed.

We might dress it up in other words, such as "Since the breakup, I've been so down" or "I've just been miserable since my knee injury." Equally, we unconsciously frame pressure and stress by saying things like "It's just a very stressful job" or "I couldn't do it—it was just too much pressure." What we overlook is that pain and suffering are *not* the same, and that pressure and stress are *not* the same. We typically see them as one because we've blurred their *distinctions*. But really, suffering is *a response* to pain, and stress is *a response* to pressure. Both of them are, if you will, *interpretations* of an otherwise neutral condition—and one we generally *interpret* negatively.

---

**Pain is inevitable. Suffering is optional.**

---

What other options are there? Pain in and of itself is *just a sensation*. Pressure in and of itself is *just a constraint*. Pain and pressure are essentially neutral. It is up to us how we interpret the sensation or the constraint, how we handle it, and how we respond to it. Without talking about people who are into pain and people who do well under pressure, we do have a choice in how we respond to pain and to pressure. It *does* require us to be able to breathe deeply and to mentally separate these dynamics from their blurred entanglement.

To experience the difference between pain and suffering, pinch yourself a little and slowly keep increasing the intensity. *Observe* how you go from experiencing a sensation to experiencing suffering. See if you can focus on it being a sensation longer, and move or shift the point where it becomes suffering. This little exercise is almost a meditation where you observe what's going on rather than being immersed in the experience. You observing your own response to pain like that affords you a meta-perspective, and it's always helpful to entertain meta-perspectives. They can be practiced and applied to many other challenging situations.

Pain can be experienced as pure sensation.

To experience the difference between pressure and stress, give yourself the hypothetical task of having to rearrange *all* the individual letters in this paragraph in alphabetical order—and you would have three minutes to accomplish that task. That is *pressure*, and you may or may not be able to accomplish this imaginary task. But once you give yourself that task in your mind, as if it were real, you get an immediate chance to see how much stress you mobilize as a response to pressure, and how helpful—or not helpful—that stress level would be. Breathe deeply as you consider this fictitious task, and play with *observing* your response—your stress response. As with pain and suffering, developing this meta-perspective is tremendously helpful for all sorts of dynamics, not just pressure and stress.

Pressure can be experienced as pure motivation.

As you experiment with your responses to pain and pressure, you'll discover how little or how much flexibility you have in your response-bandwidth. Some of us are very sensitive/reactive and will respond instantly with suffering or stress. Some of us will be surprised to find how we can modulate our pain and pressure responses toward less reactivity, and through that, toward more control. Learning how to control one's default responses to pain or pressure is a helpful skill. It can provide us with more options, more room to maneuver, and greater flexibility when confronted with challenging dynamics.

What are my thoughts?

What are my feelings?

It gets especially interesting when we learn how to separate *thoughts* from *feelings*. As it turns out, most of our "emotional" responses are actual responses to our own *thoughts*. We often suffer and stress out because our narratives are at odds with the experience we're facing. We *think* it shouldn't hurt, and then we suffer from the pain. We *think* the pressure is too much, and then we stress out over how to deal with it. Consider the inverse of these examples. If we *thought* we'd nearly die from pinching ourselves, then we would *feel* less suffering from the pain. If we *thought* sorting all the letters of this paragraph was not that time-consuming, we would *feel* less stress. What we *think* directly influences what we *believe,* and what we *believe* directly influences what we *feel.* Thus our thoughts—and the choices we either *don't* make or *do* make about them—are much more fundamental to our emotional experience of life than we acknowledge. Check your thoughts and beliefs about things. There may be wiggle room and more options ahead!

You don't have to see the entire staircase in order to climb it—one step at a time.

# HOPE, AND A LITTLE FEAR

*hope so!*" Hope is such a promising idea. As a desire for an outcome and a belief in that outcome's possibility, hope can be an equivalent to optimism, a counterweight to despair, and maybe even a virtue. Hope certainly is a mainstay of many religious doctrines. As long as we have hope, something in the future may always be better. Most people wouldn't want to live without hope. To many, giving up hope might indicate feeling resigned or giving up entirely. But is all that true, and necessary? What are the effects of hope, and how helpful is hope?

To many, hope is closely related to fear, in that we view it as the antidote to fear; that is, fear about the future, as you cannot fear the past. Life can feel unfair, the future unknown, and hope gives us, well, *hope* that things will turn out in line with our desires. It's not terribly rational. Indeed, it's rather emotional. When we feel we can't affect the outcome but very much *want* things to be a certain way, we can wrap up tons of deep feelings into expressions of hope. It appears that it helps us relax and not stay in fear. But *does* it help us and relax us?

Being in a state of hope also means we either have no control or we've relinquished it. Therefore, hope is the little sister of fear, which is equally based on a lack of control—and both are about the future. But when we are in states of fear or hope, we do *not* see clearly and do *not* act rationally. We don't see things *as they are*—when we fear, we see them as *worse* than they are, and when we hope, we see them as *better* than they are. Interestingly, *faith* combines the two, in that faith also asks us to focus on what hasn't happened yet.

Hope blurs your vision.

When it *feels like* we've done everything we could, and when it *feels like* we *don't know* what else to do, we often shrug our shoulders and turn to hope. It's handy. What we don't think about is that hope often takes the place of something we could *actually do*. In such situations, hope can relieve us of actions we either don't want to take or don't know how to take. What this means is that *hope is only an effective strategy when one is truly powerless*. Think about it. Hope can also keep us in suspense and distress longer because we're not *doing* anything—all we're doing is *hoping*.

Hope is only an effective strategy
when you are truly powerless.

Consider how you'd feel if you neither *feared* a worse future nor *hoped* for a better future. If you didn't have any images of how the future might or should be, you might then be free of both fear and hope. This would be a state of simply *not knowing.* Not knowing is just not knowing—it's not in the least giving up. And if we are *not* caught up in what we dread or hope for in the future, we might stand a better chance of being *present here and now.* And if we are present *here and now*, then this would also apply to any *here and now* in the future. Being present in the here and now—*always*—would make us more competent to do what needs to be done at any moment in time.

Being free of hope and fear is true freedom.

Consider trading fear and hope for simply *not knowing.* It's *neutral*—neither fearful nor hopeful. It's *sober.* It's not being held hostage by fears and hopes. It's calm and level-headed. It's rational and allows you the freedom to spend your emotional energy on other things—things you ideally have some influence over.

# FEAR & LAUGHTER
# HUMOR & FREEDOM

aughter and humor turn out to be very complex and little-understood behaviors with many competing theories trying to explain their various occurrences. Fear, on the other hand, is much less complex and easier to understand in its primal nature. So what could laughter and fear have in common? Turns out, a lot. What joins laughter and fear is that they *cannot* be experienced at the same time. We do not think of, or feel, laughter and fear at the same time, or in the same thought, or the same moment. The reason we don't think of those two together is because they cannot exist at the same time.

Fear and laugher are mutually exclusive—we simply can't be full of fear while we laugh, and we simply can't laugh while we're full of fear. Fear encompasses lots of emotions—with the exception of laughter. And laughter can encompass lots of emotions—with the exception of fear. Laughter is almost impossible during moments or states of fear, and fear is almost impossible during moments or states of laughter. Think of times you've fully experienced either emotion—the other emotion simply isn't available.

> When you laugh at your failures,
> you cease to be afraid of them.

There *are* some circumstances where we laugh when we're apparently scared—such as in horror movies—and perhaps we do this for the very reason that laughter banishes anxiety, thus counteracting, if not displacing, real fear. Fear cannot abide humor, and we all view laughter in the face of fear as incomprehensibly courageous, and interestingly *stronger* than fear. Laughter dispels and trumps fear.

And then there are oodles of situations that are ruled by one—to the exclusion of the other. Consider most churches and religious services—maybe it's thanks to the implied "fear of God," or "fear of the devil," but laughter is generally *not* present in those situations. Laughter in most faith-based organizations—for example, in churches—would likely undermine the piousness and rule-based obedient behavior. Laughter doesn't take anything seriously. Most organized religious hierarchies appear to employ fear as part of their faith structures, and would probably lose their hold on people if things were "funny." Fear relies on the absence of laughter—you cannot laugh and be afraid at the same time.

Fear relies on the absence of laughter.

You may have seen this in movies more than you have experienced it yourself, but think of fear-inducing situations where a responder to such situations simply bursts out laughing. The person attempting to inspire fear will simply lose their power within a second if the responder reacts with laughter. The "fearful" situation becomes "laughable" and thus loses its entire negative effect. Laughter is possibly the single best recipe for countering fear.

Looked at from another angle, people who are rolling around on the floor laughing will not be able to grasp a dangerous situation that might be present—they are, for the time being, basically incapable of allowing the emotion of fear into their minds and hearts. Even in survival situations, dynamics can *appear* to be funny, and thus bystanders who feel entertained may fail to take a life-threatening situation seriously—*because it's funny*! Much damage can be done to people in perilous situations when onlookers, flooded with feel-good emotions of "fun," fail to grasp the severity of a situation and fail to *empathize* with the fearful state of a person in danger.

Fear usually relies on the *past* (experience) and the *future* (unknown) to work. Our internal stories that compare an *unknown* future to a *known* past make fear in the moment possible. That means that when we're fearful, we depart from the state of being present in the moment. *Laughter* directly counteracts our stories of the past and the future and brings us back to the present moment. "Laughter is the best medicine" could well be deeply true.

Laughter is an excellent way to get present.

Fear of others, of strangers, or of people with more author-ity—those "social" fears are all mitigated by humor and laughter. It's nearly impossible to maintain a fearful dis-tance from strangers or distance in social hierarchies when you're just howling with laughter. Irresistible laughter is also contagious, thereby connecting people. Laughter also functions as social glue in such situations—it brings all of us closer to one another.

# THE MYTH OF GOOD GUYS & BAD GUYS

O h, how we all love to see the world through the lens of *good guys* and *bad guys*. From Hollywood movies to international military conflicts, there always appear to be *the good guys* and *the bad guys*. When it comes to "Good vs. Evil," we're almost all on the side of the good guys, and most of us are more than okay with fighting the bad guys. To some degree, our current worldview even relies on the separation of people into good guys and bad guys. But are we, and is the world, separable into angelic people and evil people? And is that kind of black-and-white separation helpful—or could it possibly even be harmful?

It may be *too easy* to divide the world into *good guys* and *bad guys*. For one, there are many shades of gray between black and white. And are there truly bad people? How many *bad guys* have you met yourself, in person, whom you can surely state are *bad guys*? Most people are neither—neither all good nor all bad. There aren't just cheaters and liars—and then all of us, the honest people. People who lie and cheat *all the time* are in the vast minority. So are those who never cheat or lie—those too are in the vast minority. In fact, with extremely rare exceptions, most people lie and cheat *a little*, here and there—maybe a little on their taxes, maybe a little with the speed limit, maybe a little with an erroneous refund in their favor, or maybe just with a little white lie.

Here and there, most of us cheat and lie a little.

If the truly wicked and the truly saintly are in the vast minority, isn't it curious that the vast majority of us are so eager to divvy up the world into just good guys and bad guys? It raises the question of how this benefits or helps us. It does make us righteous, indignant, and fosters our sense of belonging *to the right people* by making sure that, at least in speech, we don't belong to *bad guys*—but that those bad guys are only *other* people. It makes the world an easy place where we are on the "right" side. But is this true, or don't all of us feel on the "right" side—from our perspective?

This is not a very strong and healthy position. It allows us to overlook all the little deceptions and lies that we ourselves have committed. It allows us to have pictures of enemies in our minds—"bad actors" that need to be eliminated—all without us having to eliminate anything within ourselves. It allows us to see a world in which problems are *outside* of us. It stokes our senses of righteousness and indignation, it justifies negative and uncompassionate behavior toward ourselves and others, it justifies us in seeing other people as less than human, and it justifies us feeling chill about international military operations against so-called "bad actors." It polarizes our worldview, decreases our ability to remain compassionate, and assigns blame without taking any responsibility for ourselves, our actions, and our beliefs.

---

In conflict and in war, one side's *good* guys always become the other side's *bad* guys.

---

This of course immediately raises the possibility of those "bad actors" also seeing *us* as bad actors—from their perspective. It's very hard to argue that this would not be the case. In that way, we're all engaging in a game of "othering"—the practice of viewing or treating a person or group of people as intrinsically different from and alien to ourselves. Would we want others to view and treat *us* that way? Chances are we wouldn't, in which case it would be sensible to *not* do that to others either. After all, people who speak other languages and have different skin tones or physical features look just as strange to us *as we do to them*.

Could it be that there are no bad guys *and* no good guys at all, but just "us all"—people doing their best in life with the information and education and skill they happen to have? Could it be just an illusion to identify *good guys* and *bad guys* at all?

It's silly to adhere to beliefs that are rooted
in a one-sided and insular reality,
especially when there's outside evidence
contrary to those beliefs.

# OVERCOMING TRAUMA: WALKING WOUNDED

Trauma is individual. Nobody can ascertain what was or is traumatic for another person. In essence, if it *felt* or *feels* traumatic, then it was or is traumatic. Very rarely will we encounter someone whose life has been nothing but a breeze—in *their* experience. Some of us have been traumatized a little, and some a lot. Almost all of us are walking around wounded and, in one way or another, scarred (and scared) on the inside. Yet we walk through the world as if none of this damage exists.

Walking wounded, we still put one foot in front of the other, and we do the best we can. Of course we want to heal, overcome, and move on. Needless to say, it's not as easy as 1-2-3. Some of us try to forget, some of us do a lot of reflection and self-work, and some of us engage the assistance of therapeutic professionals to help us come out the other end of what can feel like a long, dark tunnel. But *how* do we know if our efforts have paid off, *when* do we know that we've dealt with it enough, and when can we move on and truly leave it behind us? It can be overwhelming and feel like being in a jungle for too long, where the way out and onwards can be unclear or invisible.

We tend to repeat what we haven't repaired.

Yet there are ways in which we can tell that "it's good now" and that we can *move on*. It starts with being able to entertain, at will, thoughts and feelings about what happened. It starts with no longer feeling inescapable emotional charges about the experiences. It starts with being afforded some choice about recalling the experiences, meaning thoughts and feelings about them don't intrude into our current lives at random. It starts with being able to speak coherently and appropriately about the experiences here and now. It starts when recalling those events doesn't entail further significant damage to our self-esteem. It starts when we can make some sense of what happened, no matter how unfortunate and painful it may have been at the time.

> Trauma may not have been your fault;
> healing, however, is your responsibility.

Those steps are *not* easy ones, but they do demonstrate that you're coming out of the tunnel of emotional damage. It's simply *not* easy for most of us to talk about historic traumatic experiences without much emotional charge. But it *is* of critical value and importance to strive toward that ability. If we don't manage to gain that amount of distance between what happened and who we are now, then we will always remain in the grip of past traumatic experiences. We can pretend we're fully functional and reasonably well-adjusted, but we'll be *pretending*. And we don't want to be pretending when it comes to healing from trauma. The stakes are too high to pretend.

Trauma can feel overwhelming as long as we leave it be. But once you have a road map and a desired outcome or state, it can begin to feel manageable. It's like being lost in the jungle and all of a sudden seeing your way out from a helicopter perspective. Starting with your honest status quo, your road map will eventually take you to your desired end state—the place when and where you can tell that you're good now, and that you can leave it all in the past. It's very helpful to invest in such a road map and to get clear about how far you want to go.

Walking wounded, we pretend we're all right when often we know, deep down, that we're not—yet—all right. Take stock, think about a road map, describe a clear goal, and invest in what it takes to heal. Map it out for yourself, share it with those you trust, and realize, most of all, that almost all the people around you are in the same boat—we all want to forget certain things, are working on some things but not others, or haven't managed to get away from being just plain scared and scarred.

*Healing trauma requires patience, gentleness, yet also sobriety and perseverance.*

Imagine a future where nothing from old traumas has a hold on you anymore, where your actions and reactions are in no way ruled by what happened way back when. You have choices on your way to there, choices of acknowledgment, investment, and work. But that doesn't mean it can't be done. Getting free and clear of old traumas and scars *is* possible—we just have to be extremely sober about how far we've come and how far we've still got to go. Pretending to be all right is *not helpful* when it comes to overcoming trauma.

# CONVERSATIONS WITH OTHERS

When communicating with others, and especially when the stakes seem high, we often fall into certain habits and traps that keep us from showing up as our best selves. We may struggle to verbalize how we feel, to express ourselves with clarity, to feel understood, and to have constructive dialogues. Some of these habits and traps would benefit from a deeper understanding, so that communicating with others can be more aligned with ourselves, take less effort, and yield better results. Here are some foundational topics that may help with communicating effectively, respectfully, and with more autonomy.

# COMMUNICATING EFFECTIVELY

Let's face it, none of us ever learned how to communicate very well. As adults, most of us have sat through too many meetings or lectures that were too damn long, not clear or succinct enough, without enough new and relevant information, and delivered in dreary or monotonous ways. Maybe unsurprisingly, this is actually a reflection of most of us: we talk for too long, are often unclear, share irrelevant or old information, and are not varied or dynamic in our delivery. So others get impatient, confused, and tired—and sometimes all three. Most times, those "others" are us. Wouldn't it be great if communicating effectively was taught in school? Imagine how much easier relationships could be!

None of us learned how to communicate well.

So we've met the enemy, and it is us! Yet, effective communication *can* be compelling, a pleasure to experience, and even a pleasure to deliver. It's particularly effective when it is four things: *concise*, *clear*, *relevant*, and *delivered with variety*. Needless to say, that is the rare exception. But it is entirely achievable. Take a bit of time to see how your communication is, and ask for feedback if you're unsure. Adapt. Try again. Improve. Repeat. Not only does it feel good to be able to express yourself clearly and concisely, but it also feels good to be understood. You will feel better and your listeners will love it. It's win-win, and warm and fuzzy all around.

Others love it (and us)
when we make it easy for them to listen to us.

The payback of communicating effectively is enormous—all we have to remember is the last time we loved listening to someone and how enjoyable that was, and also that it made the speaker rather lovable. But it means we have to *adapt*, as we've likely learned to *pad* our arguments and stories, to be a little repetitive, a little defensive, to do a little extra explaining, and occasionally include a jab at someone. It's important to realize and acknowledge that these seemingly normal behaviors are all poisonous to effective communication.

What's paramount is to keep it simple, clear, and clean. No padding, no defending, no explaining, and no attacking. Trying it, you may find that it's hard—*but* that it's worth it. Speak of your own truth, keep it simple and concise, *avoid* talking about what others did or didn't do, and don't muddle your point with excessive padding, filler words, defensiveness, over-explaining, or veiled attacks. The best communication is concise, simple, full of heart, full of presence, and elegant. Play with it until you can find all those elements in how you want to express yourself. You will learn to love it, and people will love and admire you for it.

Great live communication entails concision, simplicity, heartfulness, presence, and elegance.

It takes practice to become aware of just how much we pad our points, talk around subjects, use filler words, are a little defensive, or include tiny attacks on others without being overt about it. If there's a conversation you're anticipating, it can be helpful to record your side for your own educational purposes—listen to it and see how much you've muddled your point. Think about how you could make your point with more brevity, more concision, more clarity, less defensiveness, and maybe with better delivery. It will feel much better to you if you trim your sentences, talk less, and are more dynamic in your delivery. And others will appreciate it greatly—guaranteed!

# ARGUING WITH SOMEONE'S EXPERIENCE

Our intentions are good when we're trying to make others feel better, or when we feel they're not seeing things accurately, or when we want to mitigate their suffering. How often have you heard—or said—things like "There's no reason to be afraid," or "Don't be sad," or "Come on, you're not that old," or "That's not what you said," or "I didn't say that"? We mean so well when easing the pain of others or our own.

It can seem so normal to hear or say such things that we no longer wonder if this is a good idea. And because we mean well, it sure *seems* like a good idea. However, it actually isn't. We forget what this actually is—it's *arguing with someone's experience*. For some reason, we've all been raised with the idea that arguing with the experience of others is a good thing. It is not.

Everything someone tells you is true.
They are reporting their experience of reality.

Most of us feel not heard enough, not seen enough, and not loved enough. And then others argue with our experience to boot. This is incredibly unhelpful, and yet, it's so easy to do—most of us have done it or do it. It requires discipline to hear someone out without knee-jerk responses that try to make it better but often just make it worse. When others argue with our experience, we can start doubting our own internal experience, and it's downhill from there. We may lose trust in our senses, trust in our intuition, trust in believing ourselves, and eventually, we may lose our self-confidence. This can be detrimental to mental and emotional health.

To argue with someone else's experience is
a waste of time and can be quite harmful.

Nobody appreciates reporting their experience and having it argued with, children or adults. Most of us already doubt ourselves enough without help from others. Especially children must be allowed to trust their own senses and experiences if they are to grow up believing in themselves—the foundation for developing healthy self-confidence. Instilling self-doubt at a young age is nothing but detrimental. We've all been the recipient of this, have observed it happening, or have done it to others ourselves. We would be well advised to avoid this at all costs.

The flip side of this all too popular dynamic is simple and great: validating someone's experience has only positive outcomes. Once others feel *heard*, life appears to become a lot easier for them almost immediately—*and* surprisingly, as a result, it becomes easier for you as well. Additionally, validating someone's experience does *not* mean that we're saying that they're *right*. They are, after all, just reporting their experience and we are letting them do that. That is all.

The big surprise about validating someone's
experience is that they instantly relax.

See if you can manage to *not* argue with someone else's experience and let it be. If you absolutely can't help yourself and want to make it "better" for others, *ask* if they'd like your input or opinion. Chances are, they're okay without your opinion. And that's okay. If it's *you* who's uncomfortable with someone else's experience, well, that's good stuff for you to examine! As a general rule, always validate another person's experience—always. It's all they have: they are reporting what's true for them. An example of a *helpful* response might be something like "It sounds like you were really afraid. Wow. I hear you. What about it scared you?" And they will tell you all about it, and amazingly, that makes it better for them right away. Try it.

# ASKING WHY VS. HOW
# FIGHTING VS. LEARNING

We are all in relationships, and at times it feels natural to wonder "why." "*Why* would they do that?" "*Why* didn't you call?" "*Why* did this or that not happen?" "*Why* is that?" Yet we rarely get a truly satisfying answer to the question of "why." Asking "why" usually starts with us having assumptions, which we then project onto others in the form of *assigning motivation* to them. "I don't know why he wouldn't call. He would if he cared." We become so sure of the motivation we believe they should have that we find ourselves disappointed when they don't comply with what *we* think ought to be the case.

And when others don't comply with our assumptions and projections—when we feel negatively surprised by their behavior or response—we often take it personally. Usually, we don't even notice that we've just taken something personally that quite possibly had nothing to do with us. And as if that wasn't enough, we often go even further by feeling indignation or outrage—then we've taken things rather personally. Asking "why" bears some unsavory fruits!

Asking "why" always questions someone else's motivation, and we simply cannot know anybody's motivation at any time, regardless of how strongly we believe we do. Furthermore, asking "why" by definition incorporates speculation and interpretation. Both are terribly unreliable ingredients *if* one wants to find out what actually happened. Regrettably, more often than not we'd rather be "right" than find out what actually happened. There can be a strange compulsion to feel a little victimized at times. This can give us a warm and fuzzy feeling, because it makes us feel like we're right. When "why" is the starting point, our judgments enter the equation quickly—too quickly—and we can find ourselves taking sides (mostly our own or those of people close to us), and then we assign *blame*. Rather quickly, we'll act as if we're the prosecution, the judge, and the jury all in one. In our minds, we compare someone else's actions with *our* desired belief of what their motivations should make them do, forgetting that we're not them. We may be so habituated to doing this that we may not even realize that we're doing it. Not being aware of doing it, we may not realize that asking "why" or "why not" often leads us down a dead-end street where there's neither real learning nor a true resolution.

Most of us don't know *why* we do what we do—children in particular don't know.

Asking "why" puts others on the defense. Asking "how" doesn't put others on the defense. They can simply share or explain rather than defend. And when people are defensive, they will most often create safety for themselves by infusing their story with strong emotions that don't help *them*—and it actually doesn't help us either. It's a generous act to allow others to just *share* instead of having to defend themselves. Asking "how" instead of "why" opens up that dialogue. "How did your day go, that you didn't end up picking me up, which I thought you would?" is a very different question from "Why did you not pick me up?" "What's been going on?" is a much more welcome—and open-ended—question than "Why didn't you call?"

If you want a fight, ask *why*.
If you want to learn something, ask *how*.

Asking "how" can take the easy shapes of *what, where, when, and who*. They are all inquiries into *facts*, not *motives*. Facts are just that—facts. When facts are not clouded and infused by emotions, they become *knowable* to us, and release us from the clutches of automatic emotional responses. *Facts* bring out amazing qualities in us, such as understanding, compassion, and empathy. It bonds us as people rather than distancing us from each another. Going the "how" route rather than the "why" route brings us closer and makes us less reactive. Asking "why" always raises the stakes, even if minimally. Asking *what, where, when,* and *who* lowers the stakes and anxiety.

> Asking "why" creates distance.
> Asking "how" creates closeness.

If instead of asking "why" we were to ask "how," we would learn a lot more—we'd learn about our biases, our preconceived notions, and our assumptions and projections. Plus, we'd actually learn a lot about others. If we stick to the facts and ask *what* happened—*what, when, where,* and to whom—then we get a lot further in our understanding.

This allows us to go beyond "who's right" and it doesn't immediately push others into a defensive position. It avoids the taking of sides and can be a learning experience about yourself and others—the *system* in which something took place.

Asking "why" escalates any situation.
Asking *what, where, when, and who*
de-escalates any situation.

Using this approach, you'll be surprised what you can learn and how it can broaden your horizon. It can expand your capacity for understanding and compassion, it can strengthen the bond you have with others, and it can calm both you and the other person. Asking "how" rather than "why" can provide relief from knee-jerk judging, blaming, and taking things personally. And best of all, we may expand our capacity as humans.

# NICENESS VS. HONESTY, KINDNESS VS. TRUTH

It's an eternal debate: should you give preference to being honest at all times, or should you give preference to being nice at all times? The world can appear harsh and it can seem sensible to always want to be nice, or at least kind. And hard truths can, at times, hurt others, and we know this because they have likely hurt *us* in the past. So, which course to take…?

We don't want to hurt the feelings of others, and therefore often feel compelled to either say nothing or not speak the whole truth, because we assume that the truth will hurt or we don't know how to be kind *and* honest. And it's hardly a secret that most of us are too hard on ourselves and too unkind to ourselves. Everybody can use more kindness.

*Kindness is behavior coming from genuine care for another person's best interests.*

Yet, niceties and kindness in the form of lies—or by lying by omission—typically only causes short-term satisfaction. It makes others apparently happy for a time, and saves you from having to express uncomfortable truths. Yet, it can be the root of bigger problems down the road for all involved. Often, in retrospect, we wish we would have been more honest, had we only known *how* to be kind *and* honest. We often fear that being totally honest is "too radical" or "brutal." However, it is only brutal if we make it about others. As long as we make it about ourselves, being radically honest is actually an act of kindness—to ourselves and to others.

*Lying by omission is still lying.*

One could argue that the nicest and kindest act of all is helping others so they can help themselves, and this more often than not will have to involve the truth. While there are rare occasions where kindness trumps truthfulness, learning how to be kind *and* honest yields the most rewards. Niceness or kindness and honesty or truth are not mutually exclusive: sharing about yourself honestly and with respect for others allows you to communicate effectively and kindly.

Religious mother on her deathbed:
"Son, do you think I will go to heaven?"
Atheist son: "Yes, I'm sure of it."

So how can you combine being nice and kind with truthfulness and honesty? One surefire way is to speak *your truth* by talking about *yourself*—report *your* experience. Avoid talking about uninvolved parties and avoid talking about what the other person did or didn't do (e.g., "well, *you* didn't confirm our meeting")—hard as that may be. Consider the *context* of your truth and see if you can *frame* your truth. An example might be "I know we've both looked forward to our visit. I want to be available and present for our visit, and I realize now that I'm not feeling well enough to show up the way I'd like to. I'm wondering if we could reschedule."

Keep in mind that *unsolicited* truths (especially about others) and truths without a shared context are usually not a great gift. If someone doesn't ask for your opinion, it's best not to volunteer it. In general, first see if what others need is kindness, as kindness is always a welcome gift. Be nice and kind, but *not* at the expense of what's true for you, as kindness without truth is not really kind at all. Practicing *kind honesty* may feel hard, uncomfortable, unnatural, and can take time and practice. Give yourself permission to struggle with this. It's well worth the effort.

---

Kind truth is factual information,
no matter how distressing,
offered respectfully with a gentle, caring heart.

---

Honesty *with* kindness can actually help us to recognize the many vulnerabilities which we all share and that underlie so much of our collective behavior. Then, moments of apparent conflict don't have to make us feel disconnected, isolated, and alienated—instead, they can actually connect us more fundamentally to one another. They can allow us to recognize the familiar fears, dreads, hopes and desires in all of us. These feelings drive so many of our behaviors. While we sometimes find them so difficult in others, it turns out that sharing your *own* experience of them—*your* truth—connects us rather than alienates us. Being kind *and* honest creates closeness despite our fears that it will create distance.

Kindness without truth is not really kind at all.

# VENTING—BECAUSE IT FEELS SO GOOD!

Boy, does it feel good to vent sometimes, to get something off our chest. It makes us feel so good in the moment. It's almost like the psychological equivalent of having to go to the bathroom—there's an urge, and then a great sense of relief. But do we ever wonder why we vent, what it's motivated by, and especially, what it achieves? What's going on here? It can be a foregone conclusion that since it feels so good, it must be a good thing.

When we have the desire to vent, we can tell that it helps relieve pressure that's built up inside of us. We don't usually know what *else* to do with that built-up pressure. The desire to get something off our chest is usually strong enough that we forget to consider the *before* and the *after* of venting. The *before* would be how we got to this point of high internal pressure that wants to relieve itself. And the *after* would be what we have achieved with the venting, and where it brought us—and those whom we likely roped into listening to us.

Let's look at the before—how we got there. The pressure, or anxiety that builds up inside of us, is of a *relational* nature—meaning the anxiety arose in the context of a relationship. And *if* we feel the need to vent, it means that we feel unable to relieve that anxiety *within* the relational context in which it arose. This is key: we *feel* like we can't address, process, and resolve the tension or pressure *within* the context where it was created. So if we consider the *before*, then it becomes clear that venting to a third party doesn't solve anything where it should—and where the agitated energy belongs in the first place.

When you feel like venting, ask yourself
how this helps you resolve your conflict.

Looking at the after, it gets a bit trickier, and presents two dynamics. One, we've now roped a third party into our equation and maybe gotten validation, support, or even righteous indignation from them. While this *feels* great at the time (we were right, after all!), we now have an ally who's not actually part of the original equation, and thus ultimately unhelpful. Besides, our ally now has to sit with what we unloaded on them, and they probably didn't ask for that, did they? Secondly, since the pressure and tension *appears* to have subsided, we now have no strong need to *actually* address our strong feelings in the context in which they arose—the original relationship. So we're missing that boat.

Venting doesn't soothe anger—it fuels it.

Some repetitive dynamics are *virtuous cycles*—the more you do something, the better things get, and some repetitive dynamics are *vicious cycles*—the more you do something, the worse things get. Venting is part of a vicious cycle, especially because once the built-up internal pressure is relieved *elsewhere*, 99% of the time down the road one will find oneself in essentially the same repetitive dynamic. It may not be with the same person; it could be with serial partners. Either way, if we don't resolve problems *where* they occur, we likely will be presented with them time and again.

It becomes clear that venting, despite feeling great at the time, turns out to *not* be a good way to handle and resolve internal pressure at all. In essence, we flee the scene where it took place, we rope in third parties who are not party to the original dynamic, and we get their validation, support, and maybe even their indignation. Then we feel good, the tension has relieved itself, and we return to the scene in hopes all those bad feelings will never return—which, of course, they do.

Venting solves nothing.

Knowing this, consider what you might be doing if you feel you just *need* to vent about something. See if there's any other way you can address this internal tension and anxiety. See if there's a way in which you can address it *within* yourself, and if that fails, *within* the relationship where it arose. Within *yourself* is the very best place to address it, as it's probably *your* very own anxiety, which most likely didn't just get invented in the relationship in question. Chances are you've experienced it before, possibly starting a long, long time ago. See if you can find where and how it originated for the first time. It was probably very upsetting, but figuring this out will help to understand its origin. Once you know where it came from, you'll have a much better chance of dealing with it.

And if you're the third party who gets roped into someone else's anxiety, consider how you can be supportive *without* letting them vent and *without* agreeing with them. Both things are hard, because we somehow believe that being a good friend entails listening to anything and everything our friends want to tell us. Furthermore, we somehow believe that being a good friend entails agreeing with them, especially if they're very distraught.

In wanting to be supportive, consider that it might be *more* supportive to *not* listen to them vent. Consider that your facilitating their venting may keep them from addressing and solving their problems where they belong. Venting doesn't come from a strong place but from a weak place. Good friends support each other's strengths, not each other's weaknesses.

> Venting robs you of the power you need to address whatever is bothering you.

# UNSOLICITED OPINIONS, ADVICE, & HELP

An all-time favorite. So many of us just know a little bit better than others do! And it can ache when you see someone apparently struggling and you know just how they could be helped. If they would only do this or that, or do it another way, then they'd be happier—or the world would be a better place. We're sure of it. We want to help and share what we surely know. Small problem: nobody asked for our help or our opinion. Oops!

*Advice is supposed to work well for those who request it, not for those who give it.*

It gets interesting when we're in the position of being *the receiver* of such unsolicited opinions, advice, or help—very few of us ever like being told what to do or how to do it. Even if the help is good help, and even if the opinions are valuable, we might still automatically reject both, simply because it rubs us the wrong way to be told what to do—if we didn't ask for it. Sometimes, we don't notice what's actually going on because the advice *appears* to have our interest at heart; for example, when we hear things like "*You deserve better,*" which is usually followed by "*Here's what you should do…*" And sometimes others get righteous and indignant *on our behalf*, which again appears to be supportive, but in reality only means that *they* have a dog in a fight that's not theirs. Don't be fooled by righteous indignation!

Unsolicited opinions, advice, and help usually work better for the *giver* than the *receiver.*

Think twice when others tell you what's allegedly true for you—how did they become such an expert on *you?* Consider if them telling you what to do may work particularly well for *them;* in fact, maybe even better for them than for *you.* Ask yourself why *they* appear to have a dog in *your* fight. You might be surprised at the answers you uncover.

Why do we dislike it so much when we're on the receiving end of unsolicited advice and help? If you look closely, unsolicited opinions and help are actually small boundary violations. Without being invited, others come a little too close to us and—if their opinion or help is allegedly "good" for us—it implies that in some fashion they are *superior* to us. Therefore, on an unconscious level, it means that we feel talked down to. Think about it. People who offer unsolicited advice and help often do feel superior to others.

Unsolicited offers of opinions, advice, or help unfortunately amounts to talking down to others.

When we are about to dispense unsolicited opinions or offer unsolicited help, we overlook that this only makes such great sense in *our* world, not in the world of the receivers. In their world, it more likely than not will actually generate some *stress*, because it implies they know less, or may even be stupid. Think twice before you mind someone else's business without being invited. Be considerate.

> Giving unsolicited advice or help is
> minding other people's business
> and amounts to small boundary violations.

When others want our opinion or help, they will ask for it. Don't treat them like little children who just don't know enough. Honor the boundaries of others. If you can't help yourself, check with the receiver to see if *they* feel the need for an opinion or for help *before* you jump in. Most times they're just fine without your input or assistance!

# MANAGING SELF VS. MANAGING OTHERS

Pop psychology and most Western therapeutic approaches would have you believe that there is fundamental value in telling your friend, relative, or partner how something they do or don't do makes you feel. The implied objective is that if the other person only knew how something made you feel, they would then be willing and able to adapt *their* behavior to suit your needs. Yet nothing could be further from reality, as this would require the other person to have greater awareness than they already have, it would require them to be able to pay such great attention to you that they would catch all the times you need them to behave differently, it would require them to remember just how you need to be treated in those instances, and then it would require them to do it right every time.

Can you see how this ends up being entirely unrealistic? Managing others—or working on others—is so very tempting, and at the same time, it is such a bad bet. We've all been overeducated in voicing our feelings and undereducated in managing ourselves *before* we bring our issues to others. The understanding that our telling others how their behavior makes us feel will result in them changing their behavior is so commonplace and so engrained that we simply do it, and maybe do it for years before we wake up to the reality that the others just don't get it right, or resent us, or apparently are unable to change.

Managing others tends to slip into our relationship equations without much awareness on anybody's side, and most times we're not even aware *when* we're doing it. Many therapeutic approaches tacitly support it, thus further validating our erroneous belief that managing others is a viable step in our own efforts to become a better person. This unfortunate belief has been so absorbed by us that even when we're the ones who are being managed, we usually don't even realize that deep down we resent being worked on.

Managing others earns you their resentment.
Managing yourself earns you their respect.

It does take a *lot* to even identify when it is that we're managing others and how we're doing it. And it takes even more to stop doing it and to start managing ourselves instead. Beyond curing ourselves of the delusion that others will change their behavior for us in just the ways we want them to, there are other great reasons to work on yourself instead of working on others. Working on others is extremely unreliable. Beyond voicing our feelings and desires, we have zero control over if, or how, or when others will change their behavior. We'll be in an ongoing state of anticipation to see if they'll change their behavior, and our control is minimal at best. Thankfully, there's a much more reliable, effective, and less stressful way to improve any relationship.

Working on self, managing self, and changing self provides us with a lot of influence, as nobody else is needed for success.

There is no wait, no anxious anticipation, no fear of being let down, and best of all, no dependence on others. Managing self introduces us to great terms such as self-regulation and self-control. It opens us up for introspection and self-work—precursors for any healthy relationship. It gives us total access to the person we're working on—us—and all but eliminates our dependence on others. Best of all, it's *reliable*, as we can rely on ourselves more than we can rely on others. And if we feel that we can't rely on ourselves, then it's a great time to build and strengthen that muscle of self-dependence, self-care, and self-love. Any changes we make on ourselves can happen instantaneously, or whenever we're ready.

Managing self instead of managing others takes a ton of awareness, discipline, and practice. It can feel daunting to even entertain the idea, and it can be very helpful to have a professional assist you in the process. If you begin by understanding that managing others is really not a good idea, then you can make room for the understanding that managing ourselves is a really good idea. In fact, the only task that's really there for us, the only way for us to be more content down the road than we are today, is to start managing ourselves. Moving in that direction increases your capacity to take responsibility, increases your ability to deal with stress and adversity, and fast-tracks your own empowerment. Managing others is a lose-lose proposition. Managing self is a win-win proposition.

All management starts with self-management.

Once you abandon the deep-seated habit of asking others to behave differently in order to accommodate you and your sensitivities, you can begin the greatest of all journeys—the journey inward. You might not like some of the things you discover, but it still puts you in the driver's seat when it comes to ameliorating what may or may not be so wonderful about yourself. You might discover things you consider weaknesses, inadequacies, and flaws. But then you can begin the process of learning how to regulate your own emotions, your own thoughts, your own beliefs, and your own behaviors. Your confidence will grow, your honesty will benefit, your communication skills will improve, and your integrity will be an example to others.

---

Managing life starts with managing yourself.

---

The great news is that you will be in charge of your experiences, and those who interact with you will be so very grateful that you leave them be as they are. Traveling on this path of self-management and self-regulation will enable you to experience more ease and less conflict in relationships, whether with your friends, your relatives, your colleagues, or your partner. Individually we all know how great a gift it is to be accepted for who we are, flaws and all, and how great it feels when others are not constantly wishing for us to be different than we are. Now you too can give this gift to others. They will love you for it.

# ACTIVE LISTENING & OPEN QUESTIONS

Communication is hard enough without things getting lost along the way. In a conversation, it's quite normal for person A to say one thing to person B, for the actual message to be another thing, and for person B to hear yet another thing. This level of confusion is often the norm because none of us ever learned how to communicate, and especially listen, effectively.

Listening is the most fundamental component of interpersonal communication skills.

*Active listening* is a practiced technique that pays enormous dividends, and can feel fantastic to all parties despite a little learning curve. It requires you to not only listen well but to also respond *effectively* to what others are saying.

You may have to combat your tendency to interrupt, finish others' sentences, "know what they mean" right off the bat, interpret, or relate what you've heard to your own experiences. You may have to learn to restrain your impulses, pay a lot of attention, and to be willing to understand others even if it may be uncomfortable to you. But others will love it when they feel heard, seen, and understood. It is well worth the investment and makes for much better and easier relationships.

> Active listening means you're interested instead of interesting.

The steps are easy: pay attention, withhold judgment, and when your immediate memory fills up with what you've just heard, ask if you can reflect back what you've heard thus far, and then summarize what you've understood. Then, ask if you understood them correctly. Chances are, they will want to clarify something, and the process repeats itself. When they are done and feel understood, ask "Is there more?" Chances are, there will be more, and the process repeats itself again. This may seem arduous in theory, but in practice it's amazingly simple to pull off.

> Active listening means you
> listen to understand, not to reply.

Eventually, your conversation partner will feel fully understood, and they will love it, and they will love you for it. This is about the only way to make sure that others feel fully understood, and once you build that into your relationships, you will realize enormous gains, increased flow, and surprising ease in your relationships. In the context of business communication, this process can be adapted and simplified—and it will still work like a charm.

If you find you need to ask a question while the other person is speaking, see if you can ask only clarifying questions to ensure your understanding thus far. When you're done listening and have understood your conversation partner, you may want to share something of your own, and ideally, your partner will be able to listen to you the way you listened to them. Despite this seeming hard, active listening actually makes communicating easier, as it cuts out all the distracting noise.

> Active listening is giving others the gift of feeling heard and being understood.

When asking someone else questions in general, see if you can ask *open* questions. Open questions are *not* answerable with a yes or a no. Questions that can be answered with a yes or no would be *closed* questions. Open questions keep a conversation going, while closed questions end conversations.

Even though this seems like a small modification, it makes a huge difference. Asking open questions allows others to share whatever they want to share in their own words—which means that we'll learn a lot about them. Asking closed questions doesn't allow others free expression; it locks them into a yes-no dichotomy. As a result, we'll learn very little about others when we ask closed questions.

People love being asked open-ended questions.

Examples of open-ended questions may be "What happened?" or "How did you feel about that?" or "How do you feel about some dinner?" Examples of closed questions may be "So they ignored you?" or "You were angry?" or even "Are you hungry?" Play with that. You'll find out that asking open vs. closed questions leads to entirely different conversations!

# AUTOBIOGRAPHICAL LISTENING

When listening to someone, we must filter what we hear through our own mental models in order to comprehend it, and as an internal process, that is entirely normal. At the same time, most of us quickly and automatically seek to establish rapport by *offering* responses that indicate that we are, in some fashion, *like them.* We can *relate*, and hence we often quickly interject our own experiences or views. This happens in the service of being *alike*, having *shared* experiences, and thereby establishing rapport. Additionally, most of us interject our experiences and views in order to *show interest*—or so we believe.

When you listen to someone else, see if you're thinking mostly about yourself—or about them.

We want to show interest in others in part because we want others to show interest in us. So we listen *autobiographically*, often filtering everything we hear through our own past experiences. This is the norm. However, herein lies a fallacy, because as *autobiographical* listeners we ask questions from *our own* frame of reference, offer or give counsel based on *our own* experience, and explain others' behavior and even motives based on *our own* behavior and motives. In other words, most of what we say as listeners may have little or nothing to do with the speaker's experience!

If you listen autobiographically, you steal the speaker's story and make it all about you.

If we're the speaker, it can feel like we share something about ourselves, and the listener responds only with references to their own experiences, only allowing us to finish our sentences so that they can interject their experience, their views, and maybe even pass judgment or give (unsolicited) advice. They interpret what we are saying entirely through their own filters. This type of conversation will invariably be about the listener and, consequently, isn't a true two-way conversation. As a speaker we often don't know why we walk away from this type of "conversation" feeling ignored or empty.

> Autobiographical listening
> doesn't promote relationships.

Especially those of us who are more introverted can end up quite frustrated when we find ourselves talking with an autobiographical listener. We try to share about ourselves, but may quickly get drowned out by their own experience our little story evoked in them. We may try, time and again, to "take back" the conversation, often to no avail as the listener might have no idea that in an apparent effort to relate to us, they're actually hogging the air. While it can feel difficult to overcome this experiential "one-sidedness," it is doable. You may inquire if you could share a bit more about what you had already started talking about before you, in your experience, got interrupted. Even hardcore autobiographical listeners will be very open to such an inquiry.

In order to listen in a way that makes the speaker feel heard and understood, consider *not* focusing on your own relatable experiences—and instead exclusively focus on the speaker's story. Try some modalities such as nodding, brief verbal affirmations such as "I see" or "I understand," and eventually try *rephrasing what you've heard* so that you can see if you got it right. Try to ask *clarifying* questions about what the speaker said, and try to feed back *the feelings* you've heard mentioned. Most speakers are essentially motivated by feelings, so inquiring about them is usually welcome.

This is also called *reflective listening*—where you pay respectful attention to the content and feelings of the speaker, and then reflect back to the speaker what you've heard them say. *Reflective listening* can be summarized as *hearing and understanding*, and then *letting the speaker know* that they are being *heard* and *understood*.

> Listen in such a way that
> others love to speak to you.

Demonstrating understanding and concern shows the speaker that you're interested in what they have to say. It may not sound like a big deal, but it actually *is* a big deal. Feeling heard and understood is one of the most respectful gifts we can give others. It will feel great to them, they will love you for it, and you will appreciate it when others are listening to you in that way.

.

# HANDLING CONFLICT WELL

Conflict happens. It's always just a matter of time. When it shows up, we do one of two things: we either avoid it or we handle it poorly. After all, disharmony sucks, and nobody's learned how to handle conflict well. And often the stakes feel high, maybe too high, and then we're as good as deer in headlights! To boot, conflict brings out the worst in most of us: it makes us go unconscious, we freeze up, become defensive, aggressive, passive, resistant, avoidant, resentful, and more. All this is bad enough, so we tend to seek harmony at all costs. Often, that cost can be too expensive.

Avoiding conflict or not handling it well
hurts you and your relationships.

Since conflict invariably happens, why not be ready for it when it shows up? If you learn how to handle conflict skillfully, it's quite possible you will actually like it. Preposterous? Give it a try by keeping this overarching guidance in mind: *be tough on the subject, but be soft on the people*. Everybody's own inner critic is strong enough without anybody's help from the outside, and conflict does bring out the worst in most of us—so keeping in mind to be *soft on the people* while being *tough on the subject* is a great guiding principle.

Conflict brings out the worst in most of us.

In line with this guiding principle, here's a foolproof four-step approach to handling challenging conversations skillfully. *Always* start with establishing **common ground**, rapport, and make that explicit. There's a backdrop to the conflict, and chances are, that backdrop will reveal the common ground you share. Share it explicitly up-front, no matter how big or small it may be. Examples might be "I know we both love this program," or "We've been good friends for years," or "You and I have been colleagues for a while now." Most of us *skip* this critical first step of establishing rapport. Don't skip it.

Then **frame** what you want to talk about. *Outline* the subject and how long you'd like to talk about it. This eliminate surprises, provides structure, and creates safety. The other party will appreciate this structure immensely—they now know what they're in for. Examples might be "I'd love for us to discuss the challenges we've had with the weekly reviews, and our chat should take about ten minutes," or "I know we've had our differences about this project, and for the next fifteen minutes or so, I'd like for us to talk about a possible resolution." Now you're both set for the actual conversation. Even this second critical step gets overlooked by most of us.

Third, have the **actual** talk. Most of us come to conflictual conversations with a lot of pent-up energy, which can result in avalanches of words. Avoid monologues of more than three or four sentences. See if you can avoid saying "you" a lot—stick with I-statements as much as possible. Be tough on the subject and soft on the people. Allow for all parties to be fully heard and understood. See if you can acknowledge feelings, yet keep them separate from facts. Feelings are not facts. It's tremendously helpful to separate facts from feelings. While this is the bulk of your challenging conversation, keep it tight, and again: avoid monologues of more than three or four sentences.

Lastly, **close with a recap** of the talk in order to arrive at a *shared* understanding. Most of us fizzle out at this point, and all too often we leave a challenging conversation with no clarity about what's next. If there are actions to be taken by somebody down the road, this is the time to be specific about them. Make next steps and future accountabilities clear to all participants, including yourself. This *shared* understanding and recap of a challenging conversation is worth gold. This final step gets overlooked a lot when we think about having tough conversations.

> Be tough on the subject
> and soft on the people.

Since most of us skip step one (establishing common ground), step two (framing the talk), and step four (closing with a recap), we mostly just stumble into the conversation, ill-prepared, nervous, stressed, and full of anxiety. We not only forget to establish rapport, to frame the conversation, and to provide closure, but we are probably not at our best *while* having the talk. Most of us just want to survive challenging conversations, but as it turns out, we can easily do better. We haven't learned it as kids, but we can learn it now. Try following these four steps and see for yourself. With a bit of practice, it can actually be enjoyable—because you've gotten good at something that seems so inherently difficult. When handled well, having challenging talks *successfully* means that new information gets *absorbed*, not rejected.

# GIVING & RECEIVING FEEDBACK

Without feedback, we would all be relatively maladjusted and wander through life somewhat aimlessly. We rely on feedback in order to know the effects of our behavior, and to course-correct when necessary. And even though we're all too familiar with the phrase "constructive criticism," the unfortunate reality is that most of us suck at giving helpful feedback, and most of us aren't that great at receiving feedback either. Almost all of us have never learned helpful and healthy ways of giving and receiving feedback. This may be in part because the dynamics of helpful and healthy feedback are not very well understood.

There are two key things we forget about helpful feedback. One, most of us have a strong inner critic—we have more negative feelings than positive feelings about how we're doing. And two, when providing feedback, most of us start with, and focus on, what we think *could be done better*. What this means in practice is that in addition to our own inner critic, who most likely provides us with negative self-talk, we then get a double whammy by hearing what we could do better from the perspective of others. This adds insult to injury as it validates our own doubts that we didn't do so well, and, quite possibly, that we *did things wrong*. Needless to say, this is *not* how helpful feedback works well.

> Words are the most powerful force available
> to humans—use them carefully and wisely.

It is fascinating that despite most of us knowing this, we, as feedback givers, *still* start out with, and focus on, what the other person could improve—or plain didn't do so well. And as the receivers of feedback, it is tremendously hard to *not* take feedback *personally*. We seem to just be wired by default to take it personally and process it as a reflection of *us as a person*—which it hardly ever is. Since we often take feedback personally and dread piling more criticism onto our inner critic, most of us will *avoid* seeking out feedback. For the very same reason, most of us will also have some resistance against receiving feedback. Since we know this, we are often unsure about if and when to provide feedback to others. But what this means is that we all receive a lot less feedback than might be helpful to us!

> Receiving negative or critical feedback
> only increases anxiety in the receiver.

Yet, feedback can be given in healthy and helpful ways. Such feedback ideally has three key ingredients. First, the feedback giver ideally starts out with what they *like* about what the receiver did or does. Secondly, the feedback giver then requests *permission* to provide feedback. And thirdly, the feedback giver is tough on the content, but soft on the person.

Since "critical" feedback can feel like an attack and often elicits our unconscious fight, flight, or freeze responses, we are often in unhelpful states when we want to process feedback. Thus the initial affirmation of positive feedback is *instrumental* toward the receiver relaxing their reactive subconscious, and deactivating the trip-wire-ready inner critic from kicking into full gear. Once the receiver has heard a number (ideally more than one) of things they did or are doing *well*, things that were *liked*, or ways in which they were *effective*—their mind relaxes. If this first step is omitted, it's nearly impossible for the receiver to process the feedback in helpful and healthy ways. For feedback *givers*, this first step of positive affirmation *doesn't* come naturally or easy. However, don't underestimate its essential value—practice it.

"I don't mean to be critical of you, but..."
is not helpful.

Secondly, obtaining permission from the receiver to receive feedback is no less instrumental. The receiver's mind will be infinitely more open to hearing what's about to come if they have given explicit *permission*. Once they have given permission, their mind instantly relaxes and opens up. Such permission is best obtained by asking the receiver something along the lines of "Would you like to hear some suggestions on how you could improve your game, or how you could do even better?" Note that this language does not contain the words "feedback" or "criticism," as those words are not helpful. Ideally, this is a real question, meaning the receiver must feel as if they're truly being asked—so ask it as a real question, and honestly wait for the answer.

"I know you didn't ask, but I think you should know that ..." is not helpful.

Thirdly, remember that the receiver's inner critic is already very good at finding fault with themselves. Don't contribute to this by falling into the trap of giving feedback about the *person*—instead keep your feedback to *specific things* they *did* or *do, didn't do* or *aren't doing.* This is *best* achieved by focusing your feedback on *your own experience.* For example, "I noticed that I got distracted from what you were saying each time you looked at your phone, so I think you'd have more of my attention if I could keep a bit more eye contact with you while you speak." Keep your feedback about *your experience* (e.g., "I would like it if you're more direct," or "I'd feel more connected and open if we spoke somewhere with fewer distractions"). Avoid talking about the *person.* Keep your feedback about your experience, your preferences, and your desired behavior. Again, stay away from criticizing them as a person (e.g., "I thought you were wrong not to speak up").

Focus on what is said, not on who said it.

It is important that the receiver understands, as part of the feedback, what *effect* their behavior has on their audience. Knowing the *effect* of their actions allows the receiver to focus on their *actions* rather than their *person*. If you are the *recipient* of feedback, it's never easy to *not* take feedback personally. Rather than shying away from feedback, see if you can *lean into it*. This leaning into feedback can be helped by a few realizations. First, realize that you're the same person *after* the feedback that you were *before* the feedback. Second, realize that you're *not* obligated to take the feedback. And third, know that different perspectives *can be helpful*—especially when multiple independent sources provide similar feedback.

> Giving and receiving healthy and helpful feedback are tremendous skills to develop.

When providing feedback, it's very helpful to keep your comments *brief*—small bites. Try not to speak for more than about three sentences. Anything much longer will likely be perceived as a monologue and will flood the receiver. Always address the receiver directly—avoid speaking about them in the third person while they're present.

When receiving feedback, see if you can avoid rebuttal or argument—see if you can just say "thank you for that" and then mull it over on your own, when you're less prone to be reactive or defensive. You can always rebut it later ;-). Even when feedback was given in helpful ways, receiving it and processing it constructively is not easy. Practice asking for feedback by framing your question along the lines of what others would like to see more of, or less of. Elicit their "I" statements. It's powerful to give and receive feedback in this manner.

# MANIPULATORS ARE ALWAYS OTHER PEOPLE

Manipulation has a truly bad rap. Most of us don't like the feeling of being manipulated, and most of us have plenty of examples of having been manipulated. And most of us would be quick to say that *we* don't manipulate others. So who are all the manipulators? The shocker is, manipulation is committed by *most of us*. Say what? Indeed, there's no separate subspecies that does all that manipulating—we have met the enemy, and it is *us*. Identifying *being* manipulated is a lot easier than identifying when *we are* the manipulators.

At its absolute worst, manipulation can be dark and vicious, and can include narcissistic, Machiavellian, and sociopathic behaviors. We all may know someone whom we suspect has some or all of these harmful traits. Then there's straight-up and overt manipulation, which most of us can spot and can either learn how say no to, or somehow avoid it. Most of us can sense when someone has ulterior and self-serving motives and is not up-front about their motives when interacting with us. Dealing with obvious manipulators is hard—but doable. What's tricky to spot and deal with, however, is *subtle* manipulation. There are unfortunately nearly endless examples, many of which disguise themselves as selfless efforts!

> Someone telling you "I only want what's best for you—trust me" is hardly ever a good sign.

Many of us have walked into a store intending to buy three things and ended up buying ten, or twice the needed amount of something *because it was on sale*. Often subtle manipulation is wrapped in deceivingly good-looking "envelopes," such as *good advice*, or advice from an *apparent authority*, such as someone wearing a white lab coat with the title MD on the name tag. Businesses sometimes hire people to form lines outside their stores, as this manipulates others (i.e., *us*) into believing that the business is selling things that are either highly desirable or in short supply—or both.

> Manipulation for a good purpose
> is still manipulation.

Then there's the advice industry with apparently stellar and proven how-to advice which, apparently acting in the interest of the readers, dispenses straight-up manipulation techniques. Consider the dating advice industry, where people are routinely encouraged to change their natural behavior in order to make themselves more desirable, or to keep suitors in pursuit longer. Not only is this subtle manipulation misunderstood as "helpful advice," but it sets up an *adversarial dynamic* in relationships before they have even started. Such advice is ultimately *not* in your best interest. Don't start a relationship under false pretenses. It never pays off in the long run.

And in relationships—platonic, romantic, or business—we often have creeping feelings that we are being manipulated ever so subtly. Others may say they *need* us, or they just act *needy*, or are clearly *underfunctioning* in certain areas, or otherwise manage to control parts of our behaviors and lives without us having signed up for it. This is often done with apparently reasonable stories which blind us to the underlying manipulation. And sometimes we're simply being shut out by the famous silent treatment. Being manipulated in relationships is often *passive-aggressive*, such as an inaction when an action would be appropriate (e.g., staying silent when a response is expected), or hostility by virtue of defiance (e.g., showing up late for meetings or being purposefully slow when speediness is expected and appropriate).

> Just because something isn't a lie
> doesn't mean it's not deceptive.

Passive-aggressive behavior is often a *pattern of avoiding direct and honest communication* and *showing passive hostility*. Being on the receiving end of such behavior elicits anxiety in us because of the discordance we experience between what we perceive/feel and what the other person is saying. Being passive-aggressive is like being a wolf in sheep's clothing. It's not anything anybody enjoys, and yet it's a favorite form of subtle—or not so subtle—manipulation, which allows the manipulator to avoid having to be overtly angry or hostile.

Most of us *do* recognize manipulation when it happens to us. It's much harder to recognize it when *we* are the ones doing the manipulating. Remember, there's no "other" group of humans that does all the manipulating, and we're not all victims. This may sound sobering, but since we *cannot* change the *other* manipulators, the only manipulators we *can* change are … US. If you want there to be less manipulation, the only constructive way forward is for you to take responsibility for how you may sometimes be manipulative yourself.

> Avoiding straightforward and honest
> communication brings out the worst in us,
> including being manipulative.

What might be signs within our own behavior that point toward us being manipulative? For one, avoidance of straight and honest communication brings out the worst in us: if we *feel* that we can't achieve our goal by going in a straight line, we'll invariably come up with a circuitous route that more often than not will have some level of manipulation in it. This may be hard to believe, but have a look at your own ways and communication styles to see how often you avoid the straight and honest path and instead come up with all sorts of creative ways to get yourself off the hook of being direct, honest, and straightforward.

Manipulators are *outcome engineers.*

It's entirely human to want to avoid difficulties, but that doesn't justify *being manipulative.* Remember that since we don't like the feeling of being manipulated, nobody else does either. See if you can communicate your likes and dislikes straight-up—being authentic and real with people puts *you* in an influential position to make genuine and rewarding connections with others. If you *can* do that, then there's no need to get creative—er, manipulative.

## OUR CHALLENGING
## RELATIONAL EMOTIONS

A chieving and maintaining a healthy sense of Self is hard enough on our own, but it's even harder to achieve and maintain a healthy sense of Self when we're in relationships. While we all seek out relationships and love the many benefits they present, they often end up threatening our sense of Self. In that dance between individuality and togetherness, we time and again seem to come across certain relationship-based topics and challenges. Here are some particularly challenging relationship dynamics and how we can navigate through them successfully without losing ourselves.

# LOVING SOMEONE & BEING LOVED

Nobody's ever looked back at the end of their life, saying, "I've had too much love." Let's face it, there's usually a shortage of love in people's lives. Most of us could use more love, both receiving love and giving love. Most of us fear we're not being loved enough, and some of us fear not being loving enough. All in all, love appears to be in short supply. It would appear that none of us ever received enough love, and it appears to be one of our rarest commodities as humans.

One part of this love business is relatively easy to sort out. Tell those who you want to be loved by that you love them. It sounds deceptively simple, but people love hearing that they're being loved. Nobody you love and who you tell that to will respond with "I don't want to be loved by you." And curiously, it will make it much easier for them to reciprocate the favor and express or show their love toward you. Being loving and communicating it is one cool favor you can easily share with the world. As a bonus, it pays dividends!

We accept the love we think we deserve.

Another part of this love business is a little less easy to sort out. Aside from love being at times misappropriated as a guise for deviant, controlling, or abusive behaviors, there's fundamentally no good nor bad in love. In the domain of love—the complex emotion—there is only discovery and exploration, with tons of never-ending room for what we are able to experience, share, give, receive, and create. Yet, when we love someone, we never ask ourselves the simple question of *why we love*: Is it because of how it makes *us* feel, because of how it makes *them* feel, because of how *we* feel together, or is it because something *new* gets created when we love one another? These are not easy questions to ponder, yet getting clear on those questions can be a complete game changer. It's an interesting question to discuss with friends. And if you're daring, it helps even more to talk about this with your partner.

Love is the most complex, beautiful human emotion we can give and receive.

Many of us *wait* for love to be *just right* to the point of going for years without giving and receiving love. We make it so rarefied and precious—and unfortunately *conditional*—that we wait, wait, and wait some more for it to present itself in just the right way. But this is like saying, "Let's not cook or eat unless we have the perfect ingredients or meal!" It may be much more reasonable to *find love where you can get it*. Although love is rarely considered to be a "practical" subject, it's surprisingly enriching to *be practical* about love. Fill your love bucket by accepting love more when it comes your way—and by *being* more loving whenever you get a chance.

It's enriching to be rather *practical* about love.

This kind of discovery process might shine a light on what kind of love you're living and what kind of love you're giving: it could be selfish love (you feel great), it could be selfless love (the other person feels great), it could be shared love (you both feel great), or it could be that your love and the love of your partner are co-creating an entirely new and enhanced dynamic that needed the two of you in order to come about. It may also be interesting to learn more about your own motivation behind caring for or loving your partner. Your love for them may very well serve as a means to satisfy your own needs and desires, and it's important to not pass fast judgment on that. This turns out to be true for many of us, and it's worthwhile to explore it a little. Very few of us are motivated to care for and love others *strictly* out of genuine concern for their well-being. There's lots to discover in how love connects and bonds us all.

The potential big surprise about loving someone is that if you're lucky, your love for them and their love for you creates something new that didn't exist before. There's the potential for a love that's bigger than each individual, a love that has ripple effects out into the world. Such larger love can create more goodness and more positivity than just two people alone. Even just seeing two people who are positively and happily loving toward each other uplifts us. It's contagious to be around in the best of ways. A large and expansive love like that is worth *striving* for—yet maybe not *waiting* for. Live a little, love a little!

Find love wherever you can get it.

# NEGOTIATING THE CURRENCY OF POWER

Power between people has a bad rap, and some of us don't want to deal with it. Yet, harmony among us all requires stability, and stability ultimately depends on social order whether we like it or not. If one looks closely enough, that social order is established and maintained through negotiating the *currency of power.* This is done by all of us *all the time,* whether we like it or not, whether we're aware of it or not. There is almost no break from it or escaping it. Just like breathing, where we have to inhale, then exhale, so do we take and so do we give all the time.

Everywhere in life, we initiate and we respond. There is no option to *not* do that, and this is just as true for *nego-*

*tiating the currency of power*—we always vacillate between yielding some power or influence and claiming some power or influence, all the time. It's a constant give and take—we follow, then we lead, then we follow, then we lead. It's normal and natural. It's like breathing. It just *is*. Let's use "power" and "influence" somewhat interchangeably here.

> Power is just like our breath—it comes in and it goes out. We inhale, we exhale. We take, we give. We lead, we follow.

Learning about *how* to negotiate the currency of power, or influence, can be illuminating. When it comes to the currency of power, when it comes to leading or following, we all have natural defaults—places where we feel most at home. Some of us follow more, some of us lead more. Some of us are more deferential, some of us more authoritative. Some of us might even be submissive, and some of us might even be dominant. That's okay. It just is, and we just are. Think about your relationships, professional and personal, and see where you've observed this ongoing give and take, and see where your natural power place is. Chances are, you already know where it is. This is natural and normal.

Negotiating power is just like breathing;
it happens whether we want to or not,
whether we're aware of it or not.

As a general rule, if you're deferential (even for a moment), you enjoy less influence, and if you're authoritative (even for a moment), you enjoy more influence. The less power or influence you have, the less space you'll take up, and the more reactive or quick your movements may be. Equally, the more power or influence you have, the more space you'll take up, and the less reactive and less quick your movements may be. If you think of an eagle, then think of a chicken, you'll see that this illustrates itself easily. By default, we ascribe more power and influence to an eagle than we do to a chicken.

One may wonder about situations with no power differential between people—when we are even, the same or equal. While that idea may sound appealing, power and influence behave just like the air we breathe. We can hold our breath for a short while, but then the inhaling and exhaling *must* start again. There is no other option if life is to go on. Two people having *equal* power or influence in a conversation would mean both talking at the same time—or neither talking at all. It can't last long either way because it won't work. To illustrate this in your mind, imagine a busy downtown pedestrian zone with many people milling about. At any given time, there will be strangers walking straight toward one another. The only way this doesn't turn into a mass disaster is when one person *yields* and another person doesn't yield, but instead takes the path offered by the yielding. This is the unconscious and functional rule we all behave by. One gives, one takes. One defers, one is authoritative. One takes up more space, one takes up less space.

Now, if we didn't follow these inherent rules of negotiating power or influence, the pedestrian zone would instantly devolve into a mass disaster. If the parties that are apparently walking straight toward one another would both yield at the same time, they would instantly face each other again, and neither of them would get anywhere. As humans, we abhor such situations and course-correct *constantly*—and long before it comes to such a stalemate. We do not want to tolerate such standoffs for more than a small fraction of a second. Equally, if neither party yields, people would be aiming for one another and running straight into each other. It would be an understatement to say that this would not be tolerable! There would be instantaneous confrontation and fights. We will avoid *that* flavor of a standoff at pretty much all costs. In either scenario—when all are yielding, or when nobody is yielding—the pedestrian zone would come to an immediate and complete standstill. Practically, we will never allow this to happen. We will yield, and not yield, *all the time.* And for each give, there will be a take, and for each taking, there will be a giving.

Negotiating power is a constant seesaw of
give and take within a zero-sum equation.

While we *do* this negotiating of the currency of power at all times, we have no idea how this negotiation works—we just do it—and we are *utterly* unaware of doing it at all. Maybe we have so little language for this profound dynamic and are so unconscious of doing it all the time because we do—negotiate—all this almost exclusively with *nonverbal* communication. Long before we employ words, we are very busy negotiating this dynamic of either being more deferential or more authoritative *in any given moment* with lots of nonverbal tools. We use our eyes, head movements, facial expressions, gestures, gait, posture, and overall physicality. We use sounds accompanying our inhaling or exhaling, make funny noises such as whistling, and finally—if and when we use words—we use the volume, pitch, and speed of our voice long before the meaning of our spoken words have the impact we think they have. Words come last. Long before we get to the talking part, most of the negotiation of power or influence will have been settled— we just aren't that aware of it.

It's reasonable to wonder why we are so unaware of this. Our eyes, skin, ears, and senses of smell and taste send millions of bits of information per second to our brain. But scientists have determined that the amount of data our *consciousness* can process amounts to somewhere around 40–150 bits per second. The resulting ratio is beyond staggering, indicating that more than 99.9% of incoming information is not being *consciously* processed by us. What is being excluded from conscious processing seems to either be constantly discarded by our brain or it's being unconsciously processed. It's within that vast body of unconscious processing that the negotiation of the currency of power appears to take place. As a result, we're usually not aware of it at all.

More power is not better than less power, and
less power is not better than more power.

Negotiating the currency of power doesn't only happen between people; it can also happen between people and objects, and between people and space. How we interact with objects and how we interact with space follows the same guidelines of how we interact with people where we negotiate the give and take, the upper and the lower hand, the following and the leading. Stage actors seem to be the only people who learn the art of consciously interacting with objects and space. Their moment-to-moment, often constantly changing relationship with not only other actors but with objects and with space is an intrinsic part of the creative tension we as spectators enjoy. If there is no active moment-to-moment negotiation of power and influence between actors and actors, actors and objects, and actors and space, we as spectators fall asleep. We find it boring.

There's an appropriate amount of power
for every moment and every situation.

As a general rule, humans strive "up" in terms of power rather than "down." Few of us strive to be homeless; most of us strive to be a bit more successful or well off. While few of us strive to have *less* influence, and while more of us strive to have *more* influence, it's important to note that more influence is not better than less influence. In fact, with more power or influence comes more responsibility, and not all of us *want* more responsibility. Most of us are just fine being a tad more deferential and following rather than being more authoritative and leading. It's easier.

A knife is neither good nor bad, but if
you hold it by the blade, you are in the wrong.

Both deferring and leading have their appropriate place and time, and this can change from moment to moment, second to second. Accordingly, being more authoritative is no better or worse than being more deferential. Negotiating power or influence is a *situational* dynamic—in one moment we yield, in the next moment we don't yield. This is part of how social order functions. We give, we take. In and of itself, the currency of power is *neutral*—like air. When one is more *leading*, it only means that one is more worthy of attention than when one is *deferring*. We simply pay more attention to leaders than followers, and while some of us want the attention, others of us do not.

One is *always* negotiating one's power relative to others, to objects, or to space. Always.

Play with paying attention to some of the ways in which this currency of power or influence is negotiated, pretty much at all times, by those around you as well as by your-self. Try to notice where on the power spectrum you land by default. Play with a little deviation from your natural default "place" and see what happens if you surprise the world with slightly different behavior than they may know from you. Or simply walk through a busy pedestrian area and experiment for yourself! For a few minutes of exper-imentation, you could decide that you'll *always* yield to *everyone*—or—that you *won't* yield to *anyone* and only stay your own course. You could also simply *match* each oncom-ing person's exact behavior. You're guaranteed to have an illuminating experience involving lots of unforeseen and spontaneous responses from strangers, ranging from con-sternation over laughter to anger!

Here and there, now and then it will be mandatory for us to adjust our default power place a little in order to get along, just as we sometimes take shallow breaths and other times take deep breaths. We are barely aware of such occasional adjustments. However, once you sharpen your eye for the near-constant negotiation of the currency of power, it may become hard to *not* notice it anymore. Once you become a little proficient at *adjusting* your own behavior *consciously*, you will notice the profound change this will have on how your environment responds to you. As a general rule, if you follow more, others will *have* to lead more, and if you lead more, others will *have* to follow more. It's a constant seesaw of give and take and, as illustrated by the downtown pedestrian area scenario, it's a zero-sum equation.

> Leadership requires following.
> Following requires leadership.
> Neither one is better or worse.

# BOUNDARIES—TRICKY BUT GOOD

Very few of us grew up with good role models that showed us what healthy boundaries look and feel like. As a result, most of us have had plenty of experiences where our boundaries have not been honored, or where we have not honored the boundaries of others. Most of us just plain don't know what healthy boundaries are.

Healthy boundaries mean knowing where you end and where others begin. Try sitting on the floor and drawing a circle around you where you think you end and others begin.

Healthy boundaries ensure that you're physically, emotionally, and mentally stable and safe. Good boundaries are good for you. They establish a sense of autonomy and respect both for yourself and others. Boundaries can be about personal space and touch, about possessions and money, about all aspects of sexuality, but also about feelings, thoughts and ideas, and about time and how it's spent. Defining *and communicating* boundaries is *self-care, self-work*. Don't rely on others to set them for you—they don't know you as well as you do! Know your rights, your needs, your limits, and your values. It can help to write them down and look them over. Trusting your gut and your instincts is a good idea. When you're in doubt, going with "no" tends to be safer.

The big news about good boundaries is that they won't scare the right people away.

Treating the boundaries of others well is just as important as having yours treated well. Respect the rights, limits, needs, values, and instincts of others—as much as you'd like your own respected. If there's no clear "yes" from another person, take it as a "no." It's safer.

Honor the boundaries of others
the same way you'd like yours to be honored.

You might worry that setting boundaries will make you seem unfriendly, confrontational, or may get interpreted by others as you rejecting them. It's critical to realize that this worry largely happens only in your mind. It *is* possible to set and maintain boundaries without upsetting those you care about. Define and communicate what you're up for *early on*, and then be flexible—as long as you don't give up yourself in order to preserve perceived harmony. Most of us often *give ourselves up* in order to *preserve the apparent harmony*. Most of us have learned this as a survival skill, and then we've forgotten that we no longer need that skill.

Don't give up yourself in order to preserve perceived harmony.

Poor or mushy boundaries are neither healthy nor attractive: all you'll attract will be people with poor boundaries themselves, and then it is open season for boundary violations. Once boundaries are crossed left, right, and center, it's not only hard to get healthy again in a relationship, but you're likely going to suffer emotional, mental, or physical distress. Avoid this at all costs. It's not worth it to suffer through it. If your boundaries in a relationship are deeply violated, it's often too much to fix, or outside of your control. In such cases, it may be best to get out and *work on yourself first* so that you'll be attracting healthier people down the road. It's worth it—healthy boundaries are non-negotiable in *good* and *healthy* relationships.

# GIVING UP SELF IN RELATIONSHIP

We all know about the necessity and value of compromises and concessions. We do what we have to do in order to get along peacefully. Yet, all too often, we do this at the expense of our own values, our own selves, and our own self-determination. We often lose our *differentiation* in relationships—we merge part of our selves with what we believe is necessary in order to maintain the relational peace and harmony. Without us wanting this to happen, parts of our selves get *absorbed* into the relationship, and we can "lose ourselves."

Most of us will have had that experience—of losing parts of ourselves in relationship—and wish we wouldn't have done so. It is not easy to understand *why* and *how* we so readily give up parts of ourselves. If we haven't developed a very strong sense of Self, we don't always realize when our boundaries get transgressed, either by ourselves or by others. While giving up parts of ourselves, we may notice *some* things, such as increasingly thinking, feeling, and planning more around *the other person* than around our Self. It's usually not because we inherently *want to*, but somehow we feel compelled to do so, as if moved by a bigger force than our own intent and will. An unfortunate result of giving up Self in relationship is that we, our Self, loses confidence, direction, and energy. And with that, anxiety goes up!

Two half selves do not make one full self.

This usually goes both ways, in that both partners find that too much of each Self has been absorbed into the relationship. What ends up existing in a dominant fashion is a kind of "conglomerate" that comprises two emotionally "fused" or undifferentiated selves. Both selves often become what could be called two "No-Selfs," and the main relational entity becomes a co-created vehicle of *apparent* harmony and peace, which both partners will work hard to maintain. Yet, the cost of such a "harmonious" vehicle often is giving up parts of Self, and each person will present only a slice or an imitation of a real Self. Most such relationships at best hobble along, and at worst are doomed. We've all observed, or been in, relationships that function like that.

Are you responsible for yourself or for them?

So how can one maintain "Self" in relationship, engage in compromises and concessions, and not lose confidence, direction, and energy? How can we best preempt the inevitable rise of anxiety? Anxiety or emotional reactivity is a response to a real or imagined threat. We all know that both involve physical manifestations, such as heart-rate changes, gaze aversion, fight-or-flight responses, and heightened alertness or fear sensations. One good step to take is to *recognize* those moments of anxiety in ourselves and then *immediately* step back from them and ask yourself *where and how* you've experienced that anxiety or reactivity before in your life. Go as far back as you can—even into your childhood— because chances are, you're not responding this way for the first time. Most likely you learned this response a long time ago, and it is *there* where you have to understand it, so that you can start working on responding *differently* when *old* triggers show up in your *present* relationship.

Just because it *feels* true
doesn't mean it *is* true.

Reactivity and anxiety in thinking, feeling, and behavior most often show up in chronic patterns. We stumble upon those patterns time and again throughout life. In general, they have all developed in the emotional field of one's family while growing up, so it's helpful to have a close look at how *anxiety* and *reactivity* showed up within us and all around us when we were little. Once we can have a long-distance look at the origins of those dynamics, we can gain a wee bit of *perspective* and can begin to gain greater conscious control over our stress response.

This entails increasing our ability to think, perceive, speak, and act from a *fact-based* rather than a feeling-based assessment of what is going on. *Feelings* then become *one* of the facts that provide valuable information in deciding what to do in a given situation. This is much more helpful than using the knee-jerk *emotional lens* which colors and distorts perceptions and decision-making. When noticing some anxiety arise inside yourself, a good question to ask yourself is "What are my thoughts about these feelings?"

What are your thoughts about these feelings?

No matter how young or old you are, it's always a good idea to work on *differentiating* yourself from others you're in relationship with. Differentiation of Self includes well-thought-out principles, morals, and ethics, which enhance developing a solid sense of Self. A person with a solid sense of Self will *not* be swayed by fads or opinions and will *not* feel pressured to think, feel, and act like others do. A solid Self will be less susceptible to social pressures and social competition. This is a tall order, but well worth pursuit and investment. Differentiating yourself step by step means you decrease chronic anxiety and become *less* reactive to what others think, feel, and do.

See if you can define your position and boundaries early and up-front. Do what you're up for, then be flexible and provide options that may work for others. Do your very best to not give up Self to preserve perceived harmony. Ask yourself if you are responsible for yourself or for them. Concern yourself *less* with how others may respond to you. When pushback comes from others, *stay* the course—*and* stay connected.

Differentiation of Self is juggling the opposing life forces of togetherness and independence so that neither is threatening the other.

The degree to which you can think and act for yourself while remaining in contact with emotionally charged dynamics can determine your degree of *Differentiation of Self*. As you become more differentiated, you can maintain a separate, solid Self even when confronted with considerable stress and anxiety. The key goal is to manage your own anxiety by choosing thoughtful actions that keep you connected without giving yourself up.

# APOLOGIES & FORGIVENESS
# WHAT WORKS?

Apologizing and asking for forgiveness are so popular that we do not question how—and if—the process works. Saying "I'm sorry" and offering an apology means we didn't mean to upset someone, but did it anyway. So far, so good. When it comes to asking for—or offering—forgiveness, it gets more interesting.

Forgiveness as a concept originated in religious contexts, especially Christianity. Yet today, many of us no longer live in strong religious contexts. Offering forgiveness means that we no longer harbor ill-feelings or ill-will toward those who have wronged us. Sounds easy. But is it? When we've forgiven someone, did we truly transcend *their* wrongdoing and *our* hurt, did we leave it all behind us *for good,* did we *truly forget* about it by having fully let go of it?

Asking for forgiveness from someone we've wronged seems to come remarkably easy to us, as if we've got a *right* to ask for it, and as if those harmed *should* forgive us. That's a lot of *unchecked* assumptions that may require further consideration and thought. Additionally, how do we decide what is "eligible" for forgiveness and how do we decide if *forgiveness* is the right thing to ask for? If you think about it, the apology-forgiveness equation is actually quite complicated.

> Being at the ready to apologize
> and ask for forgiveness makes it so much
> more tolerable and acceptable to screw up.

We often don't consider how apologies and asking for forgiveness address the *degree* of wrongdoing or hurt. Anxiety can also show up quickly, as the stakes often seem unrea-sonably high—because if we *don't* forgive, we run the risk of the trust being irreparably broken, and relationships being de facto over. Such high stakes raise the question of whether there isn't another way, another approach toward reconciliation when the bedrock of relationship—trust—has been damaged.

Look into the eyes of the person you hurt
and see if you can feel their pain.

Offering remorse and contrition while taking full responsi-bility is a necessary and great step as long as it's heartfelt and the receiver believes it to be heartfelt. However, after that, if we ask for forgiveness, the burden of relieving the pres-sure of imbalance will reside with the injured person—the party who likely had to give up something in the process of getting hurt. Isn't seeking their forgiveness asking them to do *even more?* If you think about it, that looks like all the grief *and* the work is very one-sided.

For some reason, we don't usually consider the idea of *making things right,* restoring lost balance by word and deed, *making it up* to the wronged person, or *making whole.* We forget about the option of restoring balance or equity in the spirit of *restorative justice.* The burden of righting a wrongdoing could be distributed, if not be the responsibility of the wrongdoer. Think about the times you've felt wronged and were asked for forgiveness—wouldn't it have felt better, been healthier and more effective in the long run if the wrongdoer had *made it up to you?*

*Making things right* is much harder than asking for forgiveness.

Another dynamic that we overlook is that of *moral imbalance.* When someone has been wronged and then forgives the wrongdoer, it elevates the *forgiver* onto a higher moral ground. First they were injured, and now they're magnanimous enough to forgive the wrongdoing. They likely will remain the "bigger" person for having forgiven, and the wrongdoer will likely remain in the forgiver's moral debt. Healthy relationships ideally do not feature moral imbalances.

If you've wronged someone and you've apologized, consider what you could do *before* you ask for forgiveness. Think hard. If you don't come up with anything, ask the injured person to think about what it would take, what you could *do* to make it right. This is often a great idea, as it puts the injured party in the driver's seat. See if you can restore the lost balance without asking for forgiveness. In order to avoid asking yet *more* of the injured party, and in order to avoid the injured party ending up morally superior for forgiving you, see if you can "make it right." *Making it right* might be a better way to truly transcend a wrongdoing and have it be forgotten over time.

# POWER STRUGGLES—THEY HAPPEN

Power struggles suck. Most of us try to avoid them at all costs, and usually we fail. Invariably a power struggle presents itself, and then we're screwed, because in the end, there will only be losers. The biggest loser is the relationship itself, because power struggles create distance and resentment. Usually, both parties involved feel that they have something to lose and consciously or unconsciously become somewhat rigid and inflexible when something important to them appears to be at stake. Fascinatingly, we don't actually know what's at stake most of the time.

> The question of a power struggle
> is never *if*, only *when*.

Most of us are attached to being right and don't enjoy being wrong. Because we *feel* right! Unfortunately, the other party may feel just the same way. We often reason *emotionally*—we think we're right because we *feel* right. Emotional reasoning is hardly ever helpful, yet we often find ourselves doing it before we're even aware of it. Thus we don't see power struggles coming—they come out of nowhere, they escalate quickly, and all of a sudden, there's lots at stake. Or so it seems. And before we know it, we're in the thick of it.

What's at stake, however? On the surface, it appears that it's just about being right or being wrong, and often about something apparently menial. But power struggles *are* power struggles because they carry a much bigger price tag. What's at stake are usually trust, safety, and a sense of belonging or unity. When we feel that something as intrinsic and important as trust, safety, or our sense of belonging is at stake, we freak out, as the stakes feel high. Key here is that the stakes *feel* high, even though they may not actually be that high.

Power struggles can be 100% avoided.
Simply give up on being right and refuse
to play the winning/losing power game.

When you experience a power struggle in progress, you have two choices: you either engage in it or you don't engage in it. Power struggles only have losers, even when it may appear for some time as if there was a winner. And power struggles have not one possible loser, but multiple guaranteed losers: trust, safety, and a sense of belonging all suffer when a power struggle is taking place. Engaging *at all* is already a lose-lose proposition, so if at all possible, try to simply not engage. It'll feel hard, but consider that it'll only be a power struggle if *you* engage and participate. *Consider simply not engaging.* It's like magic if you don't engage.

This is *not* easy to do, but well worth the effort. Alternatively, once you realize that you're in a power struggle, you can *stop the bad game* and call it out. Share that you feel you're both in a power struggle and that you don't want to be in one. Explore what you can jointly do to opt out of the power struggle. Invest your energy into a discussion about *alternate* ways to address the issue at hand. There usually are. You may also simply *concede* in the moment, and just go with whatever the other person wants. Give them slack, even let them feel right and righteous, grant them their escalated emotions. Just because they're worked up about something doesn't mean you have to join them. And it doesn't mean they are right and you are wrong. It just means you won't play your part in a power struggle.

---

The big bad news about power struggles is that nothing good ever comes of them.

---

# COMPROMISE VS. CONCESSION

Compromise! It's *so* popular and relied upon as a seemingly necessary ingredient for successful relationships, business or personal. Few people in relationships will ever say, "We didn't have to make compromises." Somehow, it's just understood that compromises are "a necessary evil"—something we've got to accept and learn to love, because without it, we won't be getting along. But have we looked under the hood of compromise and have we explored alternatives?

Too often, with compromise, nobody wins—and we seem to think that this is good enough. We don't notice that both parties will engage somewhat reluctantly in things they don't want. Often, this means that while we appear to get along, there's some teeth grinding, and everybody loses at least a little. We overlook that compromise over time engenders *resentment*, little by little. It can add up and one or more parties often feel, after months or years, that they've compromised so much that it's chipped away at who they used to be—and then we are decidedly not happy. We may have abandoned ourselves "for the sake of the relationship"—which seemed to make sense along each step of the way. But now we are often at minimum not happy, and possibly not even there anymore—we might be *gone*.

Compromises over time foster resentment.

What if there was a better way to negotiate differing needs and desires along the way? What if we forgot about compromises and instead looked at *concessions*? We all know we can't have and do only what *we* want in personal or business relationships. There are times where the other party's needs or desires will be different from ours. But what if we took these situations as *opportunities* to kindly, wholeheartedly, even lovingly say, "I'll happily do that for/with you, because I care about what you want." And do so with pleasure, not with resentment.

We could show up for those we want to get along with by *happily* conceding things, doing things with or for them we *know* they would love with or from us. We could do things for others without any teeth grinding, any resentment, and any abandoning of Self. It would be our full Self that gladly, even lovingly, will *want* the other party to have *their* experience with or thanks to us. We could show up fully for others in this way. Full of understanding, full of support, and full of pleasure. And, they might do the same for us!

Concessions can be granted wholeheartedly and without fostering resentments.

And if we can model that notion of concessions, we'll look for it, attract it, and engage with it. Relationships *can* be built on concessions rather than on compromises. And we can rely on knowing that the other party will make concessions of their own in order to bring us joy and satisfaction. It's simply a different way of looking at how to get along. Lovingly affording one another concessions propels a relationship to higher ground.

It might help to remember that if we love someone else, we should not have any agenda for *their* life, both in detail and in general. If we have an agenda for their life, we would in fact be adversarial toward them, as we would want them to want something that they don't want of their own volition. In other words, we are only fully on their side if we want what *they* want.

This can be hard to swallow and to see through practically, but it's tremendously helpful to remember when we inevitably come to a crossroads where we and those we're in relationship with want to take different paths.

The question to ask ourselves then becomes if we can love someone even when what they want is not what we want—within some give and take, within some balance. If we're *not* adversaries, being supportive of the diverging wishes of our friend or partner can be such a great gift to give them. They will love us more in return. Even if their and our paths will take us in different directions. Sometimes, that's what it takes—even just temporarily. It requires a lot of trust and confidence in one's own senses. But loving someone to the degree that you don't stand in the way of *their* direction forward—that is a great way to love. Concessions make that a lot more feasible than compromises.

# TRIANGLING IN RELATIONSHIPS

Triangling in relationships is something we all do, yet are not aware of and thus don't even have a good name or word for. Engaging in a triangle happens the moment we talk about our thoughts or feelings about *one* person with a *different,* third person. This could be talking with coworkers about the boss, with friends about your partner, with fellow students about the teacher, or with one neighbor about another neighbor. It's something most of us do, and do often. We almost never wonder why we do that, nor do we wonder how healthy it is.

Most times such triangling is of a negative nature, meaning we'll talk *against* people behind their back. We keep our disapproving or unhappy feelings to ourselves, and then let them out when the person who they are about is no longer present. It's so much safer, after all. But one of the reasons it feels safer is that it keeps us from having to confront—and sit with—our own negative or disapproving thoughts and feelings. It allows us to find validation or empathy with the help of third parties, and it "saves" us from having to address those thoughts and feelings with the people they are about. Triangling relieves anxious energy within us, an anxiety we'd rather not shoulder alone, on our own.

None of us learned how to handle anxiety well.

There are many other examples of triangling that slip through under our radar, such as gossiping, having an affair, joining movements that are very strongly for or against something, or focusing excessively on one's child or pet at the expense of thinking about one's own partnership or one's own life. Triangling often means that someone will be taking sides, and it usually serves as a way to relieve the pressure that our anxiety has created inside of us.

So many things about the unconscious habit of triangling feel so good at the time that it's very hard to recognize when we're doing it, and even harder to abstain from doing it. Add to this that most of us have been doing it most of our lives, and it becomes clear that most of us don't recognize it when, as a third party, we're being roped into a triangle. A friend just wants to talk to us about something that's weighing on their heart, a coworker has amazingly great or terrible news, a child feels misunderstood by one parent and seeks out the other. Triangles are practically part of life as we know it.

Most of us probably grew up in an environment in which triangling seemed necessary for survival and emotional health. So we adopted it and have been on autopilot ever since. Few of us will decline a friend "in need" who desires our empathetic ear, and few us will resist the pressure of choosing who's "right" in a conflict we're being told about. It takes a lot of awareness, understanding, and discipline to resist the temptation of initiating triangles, and it takes a lot of awareness, understanding, and discipline to avoid being roped into triangles by those close to us.

Triangling appears to feel great in the moment, yet actually creates barriers between people.

While triangling is practically baked into our lives, it presents us with real challenges. For one, triangling turns out to not be supportive of relationships or emotional health at all. Over time, it *increases* the anxiety it initially appears to ease—the "system" within which the triangling happens becomes more anxious rather than less anxious. Triangling disrespects boundaries, increases passive-aggressive behaviors, deflects from the real issues, and harms healthy intimacy. Not triangling is hard, as it faces three challenges—

one, how to recognize *that* we're doing it or are being roped into it; two, realizing *why* we're doing it or allowing ourselves to get roped in; and three, *how* to stop and get out of the unhealthy habit of triangling.

Triangling is a covert operation that usually discredits someone not present.

Step one—*recognizing that we're doing it*—means understanding two things. First is that most of us are doing it most of the time, meaning that it's so pervasive that it's become largely unconscious and we'll have trouble recognizing it in the first place. This alone takes some awareness, some discipline, and some practice. See if you can identify it when or where it's happening! One easy-to-overlook place it can happen is when a parent is closer to a child than they are to their own partner. Ideally, their parental relationship comes first in terms of closeness. The second thing to understand is the true downside of triangling. This means realizing that most times it's not only fundamentally unhealthy, but also dishonest, disrespectful, manipulative, and even somewhat narcissistic. It solves nothing. It *increases* anxiety and tension rather than reducing them.

Step two—realizing *why we're doing it*—starts with interesting questions. Is it that we're shy? Conflict avoidant? Controlling? Fearful? Cowardly? Unskilled? And if we're being roped into it, do we feel "special" because someone confides in us, wants to know *our opinion,* has elevated *us* to the status of judge? Finding answers to the *why* is tremendously helpful as it points us back to the relationship where the tension or anxiety that generated the triangling comes from. It's *that* relationship where we need to take the most important steps, likely steps of addressing things directly. We all would benefit from learning how to talk about challenging matters in calm, honest, and kind ways. We all would benefit from knowing how to say what we mean clearly and kindly and mean what we say clearly and kindly. It's hard, but it can be done, and it's so much healthier than talking behind others' backs.

Who would want to be
manipulative and narcissistic?

Step three—how *to stop and get out of unhealthy triangling*— has two sides. Side one is about stopping the triangling *you start*. Whenever you want to talk (likely negatively) about someone without them present, ask yourself if you would still be all right if you passed up this apparent opportunity? Chances are, you *would* be all right—and you'd be doing yourself, those not present, and whoever you were going to rope into your triangle a huge favor. Do your best to *not* complain about others behind their backs, to not vent, and to *not* ask others to take sides (usually *your* side!). *Keep and harness* that energy for where you need it and where it belongs—in the relationship where you're experiencing some tension. This is *not* easy—but it *is* doable, and it's healthier for you and those you relate to.

Side two of this step is to avoid getting sucked into the triangles of others. Avoid taking sides, even when asked. Realize that if you become party to a triangle, you're *taking on* some of their anxiety. Maintain good boundaries and refuse "having" to agree or disagree. Stay neutral and help yourself to language such as "Well, I hope you two can work it out," or "Have you thought about taking this up directly with the other person?" or "What do you think are your options in this situation?" Be *curious,* and help the "roper" learn more about themselves by using language such as "Well, this sounds like it's hard for you—have you come across this kind of experience before?"

Triangling appears to *relieve* tensions,
but it actually *increases* tensions.

Practice good emotional hygiene and be a good partner or friend by keeping clean and strong boundaries, leaving tensions and conflicts where they belong. If they are yours, solve them yourself, and if they aren't yours, don't become part of the web of anxiety of others. It may seem that good friends take sides, but consider that you might be an even better friend by not taking sides. That way, you respect and honor both your own and their boundaries. It's both powerful and empowering!

# WHEN SOMEONE LOSES IT

We've all been there when someone we're with just loses it, breaks down, sulks, stops talking, freaks out, yells and screams, has a hissy fit, or is in a deep funk. It can feel so serious! More often than not, we're clueless about what to do, how to help. Since we haven't been trained for meltdowns, we can go into crisis mode and possibly freak out a bit ourselves. We do our best, but often it's not helping. We feel helpless—and that hurts, especially when it's someone we love who's having such a hard time. So, what should we do?

> None of us have learned how to
> be there for others in crisis.

When one person shuts down and seemingly pushes the other away, it is actually the person who shut down that has the harder time. Yet, typically it's the *other* person that then reacts to, or is triggered by, the one who's shut down. If we're the ones shut out or pushed away, it's easy to overlook the pain of the person in crisis and make it all about ourselves instead. This then exacerbates the issue at hand and makes the situation worse by presenting *two* conflicting if not competing negative emotional experiences.

Not taking things personally is hard, but key.

An important ingredient of mature love in a relationship is that when this scenario happens, the other person moves *toward* the one who lost it and seeks to understand, support, and soothe that person's pain. The big question is if you can be present and supportive of the other *in the face* of being shut out and pushed away. Can you recognize that the person who shuts down has *priority* in their pain, and that you'll have to take a number?

This is not easy, as most of us quickly get flooded with our *own* emotions and fail to see past our own issues in the heat of the moment. Yet, it's imperative to learn to be able to do so if one wants to be a healthy, loving, and supportive friend or partner. This requires learning how to *get yourself out of the way* so that you can be the supportive person your partner needs you to be as long as they are in crisis.

> Getting yourself out of the way
> is hard, but key.

Here are some thoughts if you'd like to succeed at being there for others in crisis: Consider yourself an ER doctor for the time being—your own needs and desires are *no longer* relevant. Put *all* other plans on hold until this crisis is resolved. Forget about who you *were* and focus on who you *can b*e, and *need* to be, *right now.* Your number one objective is to reach the other person *emotionally.* This is *not* a time to be conceptual or intellectual in any way. Stay out of your head and away from facts. Your inner state would ideally be one of calmness and solidity, and *competent servitude.* The *other* person now rules, and you are in a service position *only.* Your ego has no role in this equation.

You'll be in charge from a *deferential* position.

Your overall main job is to provide the other person with deep comfort. Forget 100% about asking the other person what they need. This is *not* a time to quiz the other person in order to see if what you're doing is working or not—just quietly observe how they respond and adjust your behavior if needed. Again: forget about asking the other person what they need. They are in crisis, and it's *your* job to see what they need.

This means that you're *in charge* from a *deferential* or serving position. Getting the other person to stabilize and normalize will take however long it takes—you can't rush the river. And there *will be* a changed landscape when the other person has left their crisis state and returned to relative normalcy—and returned to you. It will be apparent and it will feel good to both parties. At that point, you can show up again with your own experience, your own needs and desires, but not until then.

Most of us have never learned how to show up effectively when someone else loses it. Being faced with such a crisis can also trigger our own issues, which can make it even harder for us to show up effectively for those in immediate need. Yet, even if you do only parts of this, chances are you will help a person in crisis more than they've ever been helped before. It's invaluable. And being on the *receiving end* of such assistance is an enormous and positive experience for the person in crisis—they will feel grateful and indebted to you. And with a bit of practice, you'll get better at this awesome way of being there for someone who's in crisis. It's a powerful experience on both sides.

# TRAPS OF RELATIONAL VICTIMHOOD

There are no words that can adequately describe the pain and trauma that comes with having been victimized, be it psychologically, emotionally, physically, or sexually. Working through such trauma is incredibly hard if one is to ever recover one's identity beyond that of being a victim. Abuse often leaves no visible scars, and it can be hard for others to comprehend the damage that was once done. And having one's dignity robbed on top of the communicable damage can leave scars for life.

There are the defenseless being victimized by those in official power, the marginalized and persecuted by regimes, the innocent randomly victimized by complete strangers, and those who are victimized by people they know who initially seemed benevolent, yet turned out to be malicious.

This is about that last group of victims and malicious victimizers. Within that, there are two extreme—emotional— ways of looking at the dynamic. One extreme immediately assigns all responsibility to the perpetrator, and the other extreme assigns some, most, or possibly all responsibility to the victim. *Both* extreme perspectives oversimplify an incredibly complex dynamic and view it only in a *binary* way—by looking at *only* the individuals involved in the victimization process. Therefore, neither perspective is helpful enough. Relational abuse happens within a *system* that both perpetrator and victim are a part of and in which *both* play certain roles that contribute to this extremely lamentable dynamic.

Righteous indignation is understandable.
And it solves nothing.

We usually remove participating individuals from the complex systems they are a part of, thereby overlooking that all of us are part of *systems* which influence our individual behaviors. This applies to perpetrators and victims as much as it does to anyone. When relational abuse takes place, emotions understandably run high, and we have the reflex of wanting to *take sides.* This is actually *not* helpful as it prompts us to lose our neutrality and our ability to see clearly. When our emotions run that high, we simply forget to consider *if* and *how* each party contributed to what transpired. Sometimes, even considering those questions raises ire; however, they are just questions, not judgments.

Specifically, two things get overlooked when one only sees a binary (good/bad) and individualistic equation. One, looking at *how and why perpetrators do what they do* is being omitted. This happens very easily, as it's natural to ostracize perpetrators—someone that bad seems to be deserving of being thrown out without a second look. Two, it feels natural to rush to the side of the victim and do all one can to help ameliorate the harm inflicted—without inquiring how the victim got into the abusive relational situation in the first place.

*If the goal is* to minimize future abuse and victimhood, and *if the goal is* to prevent the victim from becoming victimized again, then it's imperative to *not* omit the backgrounds and psychological reasons which underpin who both perpetrator and victim became. It's *necessary* to look closely, and somewhat dispassionately, at how both perpetrator and victim ended up engaging in abuse, each from their vantage point.

There are now finally good studies and books on *how and why perpetrators do what they do*. They are relatively eye-opening in terms of degrees of responsibility, and many are worth reading. There is less critical work available on how the victims get into the abusive situation. The notion that the victim *also* plays a critical role in the abusive system is more taboo and harder to tackle in dispassionate ways, as emotions understandably run very high for the victim perspective. Yet, the old adage that "it takes two to tango" unfortunately also holds true in relational perpetrator-victim dynamics.

There are no victims—only volunteers?

One emotional side effect of relational victimhood can be a drastic reduction in felt responsibility and experienced power, which is entirely understandable. Yet at the same time, it's the victim that could benefit more than anyone from an *increase* in responsibility and power *in order* to facilitate their healing and eventual re-emergence from victimhood. *Felt* responsibility and *experienced* power can be very empowering, and it seems both are needed in order for victims to eventually be able to shed their victim identity and return to a healthy identity. While it may seem counterintuitive, a continued focus on the perpetrator is much less effective in preventing further relational abuse.

Accepting responsibility for your circumstances generates the power needed to change them.

We cannot make the world a safe place. We can only equip ourselves to deal with an unsafe world. Thus, the shortest path a victim can take toward emerging from victimhood is to claim two things—*responsibility* and *power*. This is best achieved by attempting to answer the simple yet difficult question of *how they got there*—and then learning from it. Sample questions might be along the lines of was anything obvious ignored; were any warning signs not heeded; was the situation volatile even *before* the relational abuse; was the perpetrator tempted/taunted by anybody; were you prepared and equipped to handle the situations that led up to the relational abuse; did you seek support when things felt off during times leading up to the relational abuse; were there signals inside yourself you overlooked; did you trust others more than you trusted yourself?

None of these questions are easy—but they are *helpful* in claiming responsibility and power in terms of one's own contribution to a terrible situation. It's important to realize and acknowledge that one has zero power over the other person's contribution. It's equally important to realize and acknowledge that pointing fingers *is never empowering toward oneself.* Righteous indignation is understandable, yet doesn't solve anything.

Hard as it may be, one's own contribution is the only worthwhile place one can look. From a victim's perspective, it's never easy to acknowledge one may have had some responsibility in relational abuse, yet *therein* lies the power of *claiming responsibility* and returning to *a state of power.* Powerlessness and loss of dignity are the two biggest emotions that victims of relational abuse report. A restoration of power unfortunately—or fortunately—can only come from inside.

Trauma may have happened to you yesterday, but it doesn't have to define you tomorrow.

# CONSENT IS EVERYTHING

Consent isn't just about sex. In many ways, subtle and not so subtle, we've all had experiences of others imposing their will on us without our consent—and we don't like it. Sometimes we don't notice it, such as when manipulative advertising or opaque sales techniques make a sucker out of us. But we never like it, especially when we know that it's happening. It feels demeaning if others force their will on us when we haven't signed up for it. For those of us who *do* impose our will on others, it can make us feel very powerful, which implies that we somehow don't feel powerful enough without resorting to extreme measures.

Consent isn't a luxury; it's a basic human need or right. It's the foundation of most healthy human interaction.

Yet, it's amazingly easy to forget about that and do things that involve others without their knowledge and consent. There's nothing good about taking others for rides they didn't sign up for. It's too dangerous. Even for you. While there may be short-term winners, in the long run everybody loses when consent is not obtained first. Eventually, the *systems* suffer if individuals haven't suffered already. This dynamic spans many things: sexual relations, the tactics of door-to-door salespeople, the clandestine online cookie collection of one's browsing habits, and more.

> The absence of a "no" is not a "yes."

There are seemingly benign ways in which our consent is not assured, and then there are serious and traumatizing ways of not ensuring our consent first. The expensive truth about lack of consent is that without knowing it, we can create lifelong damage if we don't have consent and don't respect it. Despite knowing this, and despite knowing that we can do better than that, we easily and sometimes casually take others for a ride, and possibly fuck them up for years to come.

It doesn't have to be that way. Consent is tremendously powerful, and attainable—all we have to do is *ask!* Sure, sometimes we'll earn a "no," and then we have to respect it by all means, and we'll have to move on. But if we have another person's consent, we're in something *together,* there's no manipulation or violation of boundaries, and a lot more good stuff can happen than will happen without consent. Consent is often much more attainable *if* we're not clandestine about our intentions. Once attained, it's powerful—we have a mandate, we're in something together, and we can collaborate to achieve great things.

Consent ideally is enthusiastic,
not reluctant or coerced.

Remember that the absence of a *no* is not the presence of a *yes*. It just isn't. You must go for a clear *yes*. One fantastic guideline is to only ever do with others what they explicitly want you to do with them. You'll go further, you'll go better places, and you'll be liked and loved. It's a simple equation. Checking in along the way is not that hard, and explicit mandates are powerful.

Most of us will acknowledge that in the heat of sexual passion there can be ambiguities among everybody involved. Sexuality is a complex dynamic, and we all play intricate parts in it, many of which we're not particularly aware of. During times of sexual arousal, not everybody always wants to talk *contractually* or is even in a state of mind clear enough to talk and to explicitly think about consent. Often, we may be intoxicated, which makes the consent business even more challenging. All this unfortunately makes consent somewhat of a moving target as it pertains to sexuality. If we claim otherwise, we're either wishful, idealistic, or naïve. Most of us have been in sexually charged situations where explicit consent was *not* part of the equation, and we were all fine with it. Other times, we're not fine, and those are the times we have to pay extreme attention to, so that we don't end up doing something we'd rather not be doing. That all being said, the absence of a *no* is never the presence of a *yes*.

---

Compliance can feel like an act of survival.
Don't let it go that far.

---

Consent is easy, attainable, and never a bad idea. Nobody likes being used, disregarded, or demeaned. It's simple enough to conclude from this that we shouldn't do unto others what we don't want others to do unto us. If you want to do something that involves others, be up-front, honest, open, ask questions, get permission, and establish consent. Consent is everything.

# HOW TO SURVIVE BULLYING

E verybody hates them, most of us know one personally, and almost everybody is afraid of them. Bullies. Most of us would agree that they are a truly bad idea. So how come they're so prevalent? How do all those bullies we love to hate manage to continue their deplorable and harmful behaviors? Bullying is rampant, from schools to colleges to the military to the workplace. While about half of all US states have anti-bullying laws that make bullying at schools illegal, it's still a prevalent and detrimental dynamic especially in schools.

Bullies don't bully to fight—they bully to win.

It's important to acknowledge that bullying is typically an *ongoing*, not an isolated behavior. There tend to be three typical and common ways in which people try to respond to bullying: we try to ignore it, we confront the bullies, or we turn to an authority figure to try to address it. Ignoring it not only doesn't help but actually tacitly *approves* it. Confronting bullies is easy to say and much harder to do than it would seem. And reporting it often comes with real-life consequences that limit its effectiveness or that keep it from being reported in the first place.

It's not always easy to determine what constitutes bullying or being bullied. People argue about it and about its effects. It is unfortunately not clear to all of us that being bullied, hazed, harassed, or demeaned is often traumatic and can leave those on the receiving end frozen and terrorized. Despite its cultural prevalence and widespread occurrence, the effects of bullying are often underestimated. It has very detrimental short-term and possibly long-term effects. To appreciate its effect and danger, we only need to acknowledge that people—especially younger ones—have committed suicide after being bullied relentlessly.

Trying to stop a bully by telling a child
to stand up to the bully is like telling
the weakest child to be stronger.
And it does not stop the bullying.

We often believe—or maybe want to believe—that bullying happens occasionally, here and there, but that it's not an ongoing dynamic. Yet bullies are almost always *serial* bullies, meaning they indiscriminately move from one target to the next. This is important to remember. Victims of bullying usually take what happens very personally, because, among other reasons, they don't know that it's not about them at all, that they are nothing more than an interchangeable "next in line" victim of the bully.

Some bullies have a Jekyll and Hyde nature—they may be vile, vicious, and vindictive in private, but innocent and charming in front of witnesses or in public. Often, nobody can—*or wants to*—believe this individual has a sadistic or vindictive nature. This makes soliciting help to combat the bullying especially arduous. Often it's only the current target of the serial bully's aggression who sees both sides, which makes the pursuit of intervention especially challenging.

Bullying rarely happens in total privacy—usually there are witnesses and bystanders. The role of those witnesses and bystanders is often not understood well. While they may not like what they see, voicing any opposition to the bullying can instill fear *in themselves*. They might fear being bullied next, fear losing friends, or fear violating their sense of belonging to their social group by breaking the social code of silence. Yet, bystanders and witnesses are often plagued with guilt for years afterwards for not having intervened. It's important to appreciate that intervening is a lot easier said than done. And even then, it is not a reliable way to stop bullying.

Not all forms of abuse leave visible bruises.

The easiest way to stop bullying is if authority figures such as parents, teachers, supervisors, and human-resource staff intervene. However, most people in those roles have neither experience nor *training* in how to combat bullying—or in creating environments in which it doesn't happen in the first place. So, many authority figures can actually make the situation worse due to ignorance, inaction, or ineffective actions. In some cases such as hazing rituals at colleges, where *surviving* being bullied is viewed as a rite of passage, authority figures often support bullying and the people doing it. By doing so, they are not only facilitating its continuation but are effectively increasing the marginalization of the target.

Bullying builds character
like poison creates resilience—it doesn't.

People who get targeted by bullies often have little choice or control over which authority figures they can turn to, and how such matters should be addressed. One of the best means of support is to find a counselor or psychologist who is trained in handling bullying. While that is easier said than done, it's imperative to address being bullied so that it doesn't disappear from awareness and doesn't become something we just put up with. It's too detrimental to just put up with.

Being ridiculed or humiliated in public is much worse than when it happens in private, because it increases the amount of shame the target feels. Thus, victims of bullying often carry a lot of shame with them, which further reduces their ability to speak up and solicit the support they need. If being bullied or hazed happens in a public context, the *shame* targets feel can be crippling and can freeze them in an existential state of limbo.

Living or working with a bully can be
a devastating, draining, misunderstood,
and ultimately futile experience.

If creating bully-free environments is almost nonexistent, if intervention by bystanders is rare at best, and if reporting it to authorities is hit-or-miss, what are the best options for surviving when facing a bully? Keeping in mind that bullies do not give anybody mandates to change them, the best option for surviving a bully is to *get out*—leave the environment where the bullying happens. Change classes, schools, jobs, or relationships. Easy to say, hard to do. In fact, many will protest this course of action by arguing that it's too hard or even impossible. Yet the reality is that if nobody is stopping the bullying, and if the bullying is clearly detrimental to the target, the very first choice to look at is whether to sustain more damage from being bullied or to get out.

A target of bullying is usually "selected" by the bully for their *relative* weakness when compared to the bully. Bullies have a specific "target" group. To comprehend this, it helps to understand which groups bullies *do not* go after: They don't go after other bullies or people of equal or higher "power," rank, or status; they don't go after those who are of *almost* equal (but slightly lesser) power, rank, or status; and they don't go after those at the lowest "power" level—from the bullies' perspective, they are boring and not worth the trouble. Who bullies go after are those that have a little bit of power, but not much power.

This holds a clue for how to survive a bully *without* getting out. Using a rudimentary scale of 1 to 10, let's say the bully is at level 9 in terms of power, rank, and status. If you're at a level 1 or 2, you'll be boring to the bully. If you're around levels 3 to 5, you're the perfect lunch for the bully—you're their prime target. The bully will get off on demeaning you. Let's jump ahead and imagine you manage to present yourself at levels 9 or 10. Unless you have official authority over the bully, you *do not* want to confront a bully by increasing your level of power, rank, and status to around their level or higher—it *will* get ugly. And while the bully might love to get dirty in an ugly fight, consider if you want to get dirty.

This leaves us with levels from around 6 to 8, and that's where it gets interesting. If you show up at those levels, a bully starts *to take you seriously without feeling threatened* that you're about to usurp their power. You'll become *interesting* to the bully and can be seen as someone they can tolerate and respect as an *almost*-equal, as long as they don't feel challenged by you. This may sound complicated, but it's also practical. If you play with this and try it out, you'll find it'll work like magic.

---

Toughness is not *being a bully*,
it's having backbone.

---

If there's a bully around you, and you're a potential target, there are usually three options. One, you can decide to *be played* (target of bully). Two, you can decide *to not play* (get out). And three, you can decide to *play* (rise to just below the bully's power). So if you don't want to suffer under a bully, and if *getting out* is not an option you're willing to take, surviving *just under* a bully with minimal psychological damage can be your best option. That means ramping up your level of power, rank, or status *to just below that of the bully*. It's neither ideal nor easy, and it might not be something you'll want to do—but sometimes, it can be the only viable option.

# WHAT BREAKS A RELATIONSHIP

How many times have you heard someone say, "I should have stayed in that relationship longer"? All too often, we've sailed past initial red flags, hoping that exposure to time will render them pink, if not white. Once we're "in" and committed, most of us try very hard to make relationships work no matter what. Often, neither party is happy, but we *stay*—and often, *overstay*. We give ourselves and the world lots of reasons for why that's the better choice. Yet, sometimes it's just isn't.

Many things that cause friction in relationships can be addressed, ameliorated, repaired, and maybe even changed if all parties want to. At the same time, we often feel the problems are caused by *the other* person, and yet, paradoxically, we often think that we can change things in the *other* person. Well, we may try, but we actually cannot change others. Equally, we often *hope* that if something happens—a move, a change of jobs, a baby—then they will be different—but we usually find that they won't be different at all.

There are five specific dynamics or events which can—and almost all times will—break a relationship. They are addiction, major tragedy, incompatible morals, infidelity, and abuse. We often don't recognize them, don't take them seriously, underestimate their gravity, believe we can overcome them, or feel like we've invested so much already that walking away now *feels* like not honoring our own investment thus far. And then we *stay* beyond healthy limits. Let's have a closer look at those five deal-breakers in order to better understand why it's so hard to move past them, no matter how much we want to or how much we try.

Never ignore the real deal-breakers.

*Addiction* can only be addressed by the addict—don't fool yourself into believing that you can help them. You cannot. And most addicts will *not* help themselves *as long as you do*. Being with a using addict will not result in a healthy relationship. More often than not, once the addiction is discovered, it'll end a relationship even when we *try* to make it work.

*Major life-altering tragedies* can rip apart the very fabric that made the relationship what it was in the first place. It is beyond anybody's control when major tragedy strikes, and it can often end healthy relationships. As is the case with addiction, this is often only understood in retrospect—we can often only determine what it was that broke the relationship when we look back at it.

*Incompatible morals* can undermine the trust, compatibility, and necessary shared wavelength in a relationship. Truly incompatible morals will undermine a healthy relationship and erode the fundamental ingredients necessary for a healthy relationship.

*Infidelity* is always tough, and everybody knows this. Yet, many of us try to make it work past that. Often *how* we attempt to repair it won't return us to a healthy relational state. Usually, and this may take time to reveal itself, infidelity ends a previously healthy relationship.

*Abuse* can be either a moving target or something clearly visible to all involved. Don't be a frog in slowly heating and eventually boiling water: the frog won't get out before the water boils—and it dies. Abuse kills any relationship. The challenge is identifying it, and then having the courage to get out. This can be a major undertaking.

Most often we identify and look at these deal-breakers only in hindsight, after we've overstayed a relationship, worked too hard or suffered for too long, and eventually just *couldn't* continue. *By then* we've most likely endured hardships that negatively affected our own dignity, sense of self-worth, confidence, or our balanced perspective about what's healthy and what's not healthy. It's never worth it.

Sometimes moving on is the healthiest
and only thing you can do.
Do it earlier rather than later.

If you identify any of those deal-breakers in your relationship, consider yourself lucky while unlucky: you've identified what keeps you from flourishing, and you can save yourself months and years of agony, trying everything, and—in the end—*failing*. There's no need for you to fail when your partner failed or the relationship just failed. It happens. When you see it, get out, lick your wounds, and move on.

# CONCLUSION

Thank you for taking the time to perhaps find better ways to relate to yourself and to others for the sake of everybody's awareness, mindfulness, and emotional and mental well-being. Some topics you may have never thought about but might find yourself stimulated to entertain them now. Maybe some topics resonate with you strongly and allow you to think and behave in healthier ways, enabling you to do the right thing when it matters. You might find yourself returning to some of these topics time and again and may share some of them with your partner or with others you care about.

If some perspectives challenge your established opinions, or challenge the established and generally adopted understanding of things, check in with your own experience and observation before you rule something out. Have an improved conversation with yourself! It's also always a great idea to ask those you trust and respect what they think, have experienced, or have observed. Have a new kind of conversation with those around you, so that we may all expand our horizons and positively impact ourselves and those we care about!

And finally, if you can think of other topics you wish were included in this book, or if you have unique observations and differing experiences with certain topics, or if you have any examples of how you positively applied some of the book's content, do reach out and let Peter know. He will respond.

succeedmore@solutionbydesign.com

www.solutionbydesign.com/succeedmore

# ABOUT THE AUTHOR

Peter N. Fahrenkamp, MA, has helped people be more successful at who they are and what they do both at work and at home for three decades. His sage perspective on interpersonal and organizational matters shines a clarifying and relieving light on the dynamics we all want to get better at and strive to master both at work and at home.

Born and raised in Germany, Peter has been based in the US since 1986. His Master's degree in Organizational Development and Social Transformation has contributed to his in-depth lifelong study of social psychology with a focus on self-improvement, effective communication, and better relationships.

Working as a professional coach with clients anywhere in the world, Peter's mission is to effect game-changing insights and personal breakthroughs. Only working with a handful of clients at any one time, he accompanies them closely on their path to conquering their challenges in business or personal matters.

Peter supports questioning the status quo, radical responsibility, life-changing self-work, and philosophical conversations about the human condition. When he's not working with clients, writing, or doing research, he enjoys staying strong by riding waves or going on long hikes.